MARRIAGE

*Break Free from the Negative Sexual
Script and Improve the Sexual and
Emotional Quality of Your Relationship*

DR. FREDERICK D. MONDIN

iUniverse, Inc.
Bloomington

Erotic Marriage
Break Free from the Negative Sexual Script and Improve the Sexual and Emotional Quality of Your Relationship

iUniverse books may be ordered through booksellers or by contacting:

iUniverse
1663 Liberty Drive
Bloomington, IN 47403
www.iuniverse.com
1-800-Authors (1-800-288-4677)

Because of the dynamic nature of the Internet, any Web addresses or links contained in this book may have changed since publication and may no longer be valid. The views expressed in this work are solely those of the author and do not necessarily reflect the views of the publisher, and the publisher hereby disclaims any responsibility for them.

ISBN: 978-1-4502-6641-3 (pbk)
ISBN: 978-1-4502-6642-0 (cloth)
ISBN: 978-1-4502-6643-7 (ebk)

Library of Congress Control Number: 2010915834

Printed in the United States of America

iUniverse rev. date: 1/24/11

Contents

Acknowledgments

From the inception, my partner in life and in marriage, Dr. Joan Henderson, was an enormous help to the completion of this project. She very patiently gave me superb insight and advice. Her contributions were numerous and at times poignant. Joan has been a loving partner for thirty-five years. She has always complimented me and validated my abilities. Moreover, she is one of those rare people with the ability to see clearly into the nature of things. She has been my inspiration and the love of my life. She is my best friend. Without her, this book would not have been written.

I also wish to acknowledge two of my oldest friends who never stopped encouraging me to write, Dr. Fredric Jones and Jolynne Jones. Their support was a constant foundation of confidence that I truly appreciate. They were often my best resource for answers to my questions. They are two of the most intelligent and positively oriented people I know.

I want to thank Tom McIntyre who helped me set up several workshops, including one on sexuality. His constant suggestions and encouragement planted a seed in my psyche that germinated into this book.

I wish to thank Dr. Edward Bridges, MD, for always being such a great friend. He has been a supportive and insightful consultant on any life issue. Edward kept me laughing whenever the situation was becoming too serious and intense.

My children, Julie Mondin and Dr. Greg Mondin, have consistently been advocates for my success. I thank them both for helping me to mature.

Lastly, I wish to thank Boise State University and the psychology department for giving me the opportunity to teach a difficult subject to wonderfully bright students. In my twenty-five years of teaching human sexuality for Boise State, the university has been the pinnacle of academic freedom.

Introduction

How I Learned about Sex

In my family, the one subject never discussed was sex. I cannot remember the word "sex" ever being mentioned, except for a few times when I asked a question about that word and was quickly rebuked. When I was sixteen years old, I asked my dad why he had not told me anything about sex. He became angry immediately. He responded, "Nobody appreciates what I do around here." He then walked out of the house and drove off in the car.

With my mother, not only was the subject of sex taboo, but just saying the word would bring on her wrath. Sex to her was something sinful and evil. Once she overheard me say a sexually slang word. I did not know what the word meant, but when my mother heard me say it, she washed my mouth out with soap and sent me to bed without dinner. She never did tell me what the word meant or why it was so offensive.

While growing up, sex was always a mystery to me. My peers talked about sex all the time. They seemed to know what they were talking about. They would mention some girl in the neighborhood and talk about "screwing" her. I had no idea what they meant.

When I started high school, I learned what sex was from my peers. Although I felt a strong attraction to girls, I was afraid of them. What I really feared was my sexuality. I had been given so many negative messages from my home and my church, that I felt it was sinful. My mother had somehow convinced me to never have sex with a girl. She had put the message in my psyche that it was wrong to have sex. I felt like girls were dangerous to my moral upbringing. When around them, I felt vulnerable and tongue-tied.

My story might sound extreme, but it is not unlike countless stories I have heard from my students and clients. Here are just a few of the comments I have heard from them:

"My first sexual encounter was disastrous! All I remember is that I felt guilty, dirty, and cheap."

"In my house we never talked about sex. My parents could not talk about the subject. It was as if sex did not exist. I learned about it from my first boyfriend."

"In the eleven years I have been married, I have never been in the bathroom with my husband, nor have I ever seen him undress in front of me. He is a good Catholic boy and does not want me to see his genitals or even touch them. We have never had oral sex. When we do have sex, it is always at night in the dark with the lights out, and under the covers. I am sure it doesn't last more than five minutes."

"I always had an open ear for anything about sex, but all I ever heard was how naughty it was."

"I was raised in complete sexual ignorance. My first sexual education was finding my dad's porn magazines and looking at them. I did steal a couple for myself, which I kept hidden."

"My parents never taught me anything. I learned about sex from an older girl who rather seduced me. After that, I learned from experimentation with whatever girl I could get to experiment with me."

What You Will Learn from This Book

Teaching human sexuality for twenty-five years has finally given me the sex education I needed when I was sixteen. I wrote this book to pass on to the reader some of the insights and knowledge that I have learned. While I think anyone who reads this book will learn valuable information from its pages, I have focused it to apply primarily to couples. I discuss the subjects of sex addiction, masturbation, female orgasm, erotica, pornography, infidelity, making emotional love, and romancing in a relationship. It is my assumption that you will not only acquire some knowledge from these pages but also be inspired.

In addition, it exposes the sexual legacy America inherited, which creates and perpetuates a continuing negative sexual belief system. Much of this legacy has reinforced, for generations of Americans, a negative and restrictive view of sexuality. This book will challenge traditional ideas and beliefs that continue to create fear, guilt, and shame. These negative views have stifled and repressed our own erotic expression. They have taken a toll especially in marriage, where couples restrict sexual communication and activity out of fear of doing or saying something believed to be wrong.

Western Civilization has a sexual legacy, written by powerful men who controlled the beliefs of the Church. These men feared sexuality as something so sinful that it could deprive one of entering into heaven, and it could condemn one's soul to hell. These particular men remained celibate, condemned sex, and taught that sex was only for procreation. Their biased view influenced their interpretation of the Bible regarding sexuality.

In America today, the sexual beliefs of the first one thousand years of the Christian era are still in vogue. These teachings are woven into our laws, our beliefs, and the sexual practices within the American culture.[1]

The view in this book describes a positive perspective on sexuality. Information on the subjects of female orgasm and male sexual functioning will make it clear how couples can improve their sexual experience. In my marriage counseling practice, I continue to have couples confess that they are not meeting each other's sexual needs. They also feel that when they do have sex it is not very exciting. The information in this book will help couples improve their sexual success and pleasure. It will describe how to make your relationship more erotic, and how to increase emotional intimacy with your partner.

Unlike some countries, we do not get comprehensive sex education in American culture. While there has been profound improvement since the 1950s, it is still difficult for most people, especially couples, to be open and frank about their sexual needs and feelings. Even to ask questions about sex is uncomfortable. Most parents are still uncertain about what to tell their children. Couples who have been married for years find it nearly impossible to address sexual issues with each other. Many women are still faking orgasms, and many men worry about their sexual performance.[2] The use of sexual slang or erotic language is often foreign to many couples. They maintain a low level of eroticism and sexual excitement in their relationship.

My interest in learning about human sexuality actually began in my early academic experience. While pursuing my undergraduate degree from Whitworth University, I enrolled in a sociology class. The professor gave the class an assignment to choose a subject, read all the research available on the subject, and write a report on our findings. I chose the subject of female orgasm among married women in the United States. This was in 1956, and I was amazed that the consensus of all the studies indicated that between 85 and 95 percent of American married women were nonorgasmic. They had never experienced an orgasm. Of the 5 to 15 percent of women who had experienced orgasm, it was only occasionally: 10 percent of the times they had intercourse. I remember that I wondered why this was such a difficult problem for women. How could so many married women be unable to enjoy this basic human pleasure? Males did not seem to have any difficulty reaching orgasm. I now know why it was such a problem for women. After reading this book, you will also know.

Fortunately, sexual science has now established the information that enables all women to enjoy the pleasure of having an orgasm, but to do so requires a woman to allow herself to be stimulated into a deep erotic state. Many women have difficulty with lust or intense sexual desire. Chapter four, "Female Orgasm: Surrendering to Lust," will address this issue in fine detail. Other chapters will focus on making your relationship more erotic and deepening your emotional connection to your partner.

About The Author

After receiving a BA from Whitworth, I pursued graduate studies at Princeton Theological Seminary. After completing a year of study at Princeton, I transferred to San Francisco Theological Seminary and completed a master's degree in divinity studies. The seminary was a profound learning experience. Studying the Bible and theology with internationally recognized scholars was one of the most meaningful and helpful experiences of my life.

I became ordained as a Presbyterian minister and acquired a position with a Presbyterian church in Southern California. My pastoral duties included ministering to families with problems in daily living. I soon became overwhelmed with the number of people from the congregation who sought me out for marriage counseling, which often included problems in the area of sexuality. Realizing that I needed further training, I enrolled in and completed a master's degree in psychology at Pepperdine University. Concurrent with those studies, I was accepted into an internship at the American Institute of Family Relations in Los Angeles. Not only did I receive training in marriage and family therapy at the institute, but I also received significant training working with couples that had problems with sexual dysfunction.

It was in the training program that I met Arnold Kegel, MD. Dr. Kegel shared his research on his discoveries about female orgasm and the relationship of the pubococcygeus muscle to sexual functioning. He was extraordinary as a person and as a teacher. Dr. Kegel was more than generous in sharing his research; he was impassioned about it. He believed that the primary treatment women needed in order to become orgasmic was education about their bodies and their sexual physiology. In his research, he took one thousand women who had never experienced an orgasm and educated them about the process required to reach orgasm. Six hundred and fifty, or 65 percent, of these women experienced their first orgasm.[3] This was remarkable given that, during that time, the "cure" for being nonorgasmic was years of psychoanalysis.

I resigned from the church in good standing to pursue a private practice as a California-licensed marriage and family therapist. I was also invited to join the training staff at the American Institute of Family Relations to become the internship group therapy leader and a staff counselor.

Dr. Paul Popenoe, founder of the American Institute of Family Relations, had a column in the *Ladies Home Journal* magazine, captioned "Can This Marriage Be Saved?" He arranged to have one of my successful marriage counseling cases published in the column.[4] This brought couples into my practice both locally and from other states for marital and sexual counseling.

I moved to Boise, Idaho, where I initially practiced in a mental health center as a psychologist on the staff. After two years of experience at the mental health clinic, I left to pursue and complete a doctorate in counseling at the University of Northern Colorado. Returning to Boise, I eventually started another private practice of marriage and family counseling with my partner in marriage, Dr. Joan Henderson.

My training has included studies with Arnold Kegel, MD; Wardel Pomeroy, PhD, who was Alfred Kinsey's associate; and Masters and Johnson, who developed sex therapy as a treatment for sexual dysfunction. I have also studied with numerous recognized "masters" in the field, such as Carl Whitaker, MD; Salvadore Minuchin; Morton Lieberman; Virginia Satir; Albert Ellis; Laura Perls; Eric Berne; Jay Haley; Erving and Miriam Polster; Irving Yalom; and many others. Since 1985 I have been an adjunct instructor in human sexuality at Boise State University and in private practice as a marriage and sexuality counselor for more than thirty years. I continue to teach human sexuality at Boise State University and practice privately as a marriage, family, and sex counselor.

This book is a product of what I have studied and learned from my academic investigations and my clinical practice. I have not excluded my own judgment and opinion, nor the experience and feelings of others who have confided in me and engaged me in serious discussion. The information in this book is written to help couples improve both their marital relationship and their sexual relationship. Hopefully, it will enhance the reader's self-understanding of sexuality, as well as contribute to a deeper knowledge of how to achieve a more positive and healthy sexuality.

Chapter One:

Guess Who Is Controlling Our Sex Life?

In 1996, in the small town of Emmett, Idaho, the local sheriff arrested three pregnant teenage girls and their boyfriends. They were all charged under Idaho's fornication law. This law, which is still on the books, makes it a crime for anyone to have sex outside of marriage. It is also against the law in Idaho for anyone to have oral-genital contact, even if you are a married couple.[5]

A mother looks out her kitchen window and sees her three-year-old daughter lying on the lawn with her pants off, and she is masturbating herself and singing. The mother runs out to her yelling, "Shame, shame on you!" She grabs her daughter by the arm and starts to spank her on her bottom. The mother is frightened and angry. Her daughter is alarmed and scared. She screams as her mother takes her into the house and makes her go directly to bed.

A father hears his ten-year-old son say the word "fuck" and is enraged. He grabs his son shouting at him, "What did I hear you say? No son of mine is going to talk like that; you get into the house right now, young man!" The boy is scared and runs into the house crying. The father washes his son's mouth out with soap and sends him to his room for the rest of the day.

A woman who has been married for twenty years admits to her counselor that she is uncomfortable undressing in front of her husband. She only has sex when he insists they "do it." She always feels guilty afterward. She does not enjoy sex and never initiates it.

In Wyoming, a young homosexual male is tied to a fence and beaten to death. The heterosexual boys who are responsible for this crime killed him just because he was gay.[6]

The government of the United States spends millions of tax payers' dollars every year to support abstinence education, even though they have excellent research from the country's best universities that abstinence from sex until one gets married does not work for the vast majority of our society.[7]

All these stories exemplify how negative teachings about sexuality are embedded in our laws, our government, and our lives. Psychotherapist Eric Berne coined the term "scripting" as an unconscious process that governs the way we live our lives.[8] Social scripting comes from what we read, hear, and learn from our parents, authority figures, institutions, and messages from our culture. When it comes to the subject of sexuality, many Americans are confused about what is right and what is wrong. They have been "scripted" with contradictory messages. This creates difficulty for couples in communicating about sex with each other and their children. Lust is defined in the dictionary as "intense sexual feeling."[9] While we all have intense sexual feelings, we have been scripted to believe that those feelings are sinful. Many Americans believe that looking at any pictures or videos of couples having sex is not only wrong, but also unhealthy and dangerous to one's morality.

How the Church Gained Control of Our Sex Life

Let the reader understand that I am not anti-Christianity or against any religion. In fact, Christianity was very helpful to me for a period of my life. I know that Christianity has helped countless numbers of people. I believe that all religions help people, and that is why all religions have followers. I recognize that in the United States the Christian church is usually the only place people who want a spiritual life know where to go. I know that the Christian church has been immensely helpful and charitable. I also recognize that people find social and spiritual meaning in Christianity. My own Christian experience was lifesaving and helpful to my development as a person. I am not for getting rid of Christianity or the church.

With that having been said, it is also true that nothing in the world is perfect, especially when it comes to human beings. Since all religions are a congregation of imperfect people, and imperfect people administrate them, it stands to reason that the church is imperfect in some of its thinking and beliefs. In order to understand how America's negative sexual script evolved and how it has influenced our sexual practices, we must examine our historical and cultural roots. America has a sexual legacy created primarily by three men: Saint Paul, Saint Augustine, and Saint Thomas Aquinas. This legacy was derived originally from Saint Paul's teachings in the New Testament and Saint Augustine's interpretation of the Old Testament story of Adam and Eve. Augustine's teachings were further expanded by Saint Thomas Aquinas. During the Middle Ages, the Roman Catholic Church adopted these teachings of Saint Paul, Saint Augustine, and Saint Thomas Aquinas, and made them official doctrine on sexuality. In doing so, these teachings became the sexual script for all of Western Civilization. Saint Paul's, Saint Augustine's, and Saint Thomas Aquinas's teachings are actually present today in our attitudes, behaviors, laws, and approach to sexuality. Saint Paul, Saint Augustine, and Saint Aquinas are the original authors of misogyny, of the guilt, fear, and shame with which we struggle in America today.[10]

The Integration of Sexuality and Spirituality

Before examining these underpinnings of Western thought in depth, it is first essential to excavate ideas from an even earlier time. Archeologists have unearthed evidence of an Egyptian creation story that precedes the biblical creation story found in the Book of Genesis by more than a thousand years.[11]

The Egyptian creation story teaches that the god Atum created the world. The Egyptians believed that Atum masturbated. From his ejaculate was born a goddess named Tefnut and a god named Shu. Tefnut then made the atmosphere under the earth, and Shu made the atmosphere above the earth. Then Shu and Tefnut had sexual intercourse and gave birth to a god named Geb and a goddess named Nut. Geb created the earth, and Nut created the heavens and the sky. Geb and Nut had sexual intercourse and gave birth to Osiris and Isis. Osiris and Isis had sex and gave birth to Horus. This process of a god and a goddess having sex and giving birth to another set of deities, all of whom are responsible for creating some part of the universe, proceeded until all of creation was completed.[12] In other words, the Egyptians could only understand creation as something sexual. They understood that only sex created life. They believed there had to be both male and female gods and goddesses in order to have creation. Their religious beliefs did not separate sex from spirituality. Sex and spirituality were one. They were together. There was no separation of the body from the spirit. Furthermore, sexuality was an important part of their religious practices. Since the gods were sexual, sexuality was always a spiritual act blessed by the gods. Sex was not hidden. It was very public. There was no shame or guilt. There was no embarrassment and no concept of sin. Sex was at the center of their spiritual life. They even believed that when they died, they would have sex in the afterlife. They had a celebration ritual for masturbation since the god Atum started creation through masturbation. There was no punishment for any sexual activity. Sex and the gods were inseparable and religious rituals were both spiritual and sexual.[13]

It is important to recognize the differences between this Egyptian creation saga and the Old Testament version of the beginning of creation found in the book of Genesis. In the Genesis story, the first two human beings, Adam and Eve, who were made by God, were living in a Garden of Paradise. They were told by God not to eat the fruit of the knowledge of good and evil. Eve ate the fruit after the serpent prompted her to do it. It is often interpreted that the serpent is a symbol for Satan in disguise. The association of Eve having a relationship with the devil helped inspire the witch hunts in the later centuries. Eve gave the fruit to Adam to eat. Afterward, they were ashamed and hid from God, covering their bodies. When God discovered that they ate the fruit, he became angry and punished them.[14]

Saint Augustine taught that the sin of Adam and Eve was that they had sexual intercourse. According to Augustine, God punished them for having sex.[15] They were thrown out of the Garden of Paradise. God also said that because they had done this, men would have to labor and work hard all of their lives, and women would have pain in childbirth.[16] The Church blamed Eve for the downfall of mankind. The early Christian writers wrote about her as being a libidinous temptress and a seducer of Adam. She was condemned as sinful and evil.[17] Women were taught that it was immoral and sinful for them to ever be like Eve.

Mary, the mother of Jesus, who is often referred to as the Mother of God, was set up in contrast to Eve.[18] Mary was described as a virgin who would never have sex and was always chaste. This poignant teaching directed toward women has contributed to their difficulties in eroticism and sexuality. While you can imagine Eve having an orgasm, it would be an outrage to even think that Mary the Mother of God would ever be interested in having a climax. Women have been taught to be the guardians of morality. For them to lose their virginity outside of marriage condemns them as "sisters of Eve." They are easily labeled as a slut or a whore for being sexual. This saga has been used as support for the false belief that women are the weaker gender and weaker morally. Women have to be careful about their sexuality and their reputations. They do not want to be identified with Eve's reputation as being lascivious and lustful.

Contrast the Genesis story with the Egyptian story. They are diametrically opposite in what they each say about sexuality. In the Egyptian story, creation starts with a very positive sexual script that connects sex and spirituality together.[19] In the biblical creation story, sex is sinful and separate from spirituality.[20] The Egyptian creation story gives the female an important place in the creation of the universe. It cannot be completed without women goddesses. The Egyptians eventually made Isis their mother goddess of love.[21]

In the biblical creation story, the female is not made in the image of God. Only Adam, the male, is made in the image of God! The female is made from the rib of the male. She is given lesser status than the male. In fact, Genesis states that she is created as a helpmate for Adam. She is to serve Adam. Eve is blamed for causing Adam to sin and is made responsible for causing God to kick them out of the Garden of Paradise.[22]

Throughout the Christian tradition, women have not been given the status of men nor the power that is given to males. There has always been an underlying distrust of women because of Eve. Saint Thomas Aquinas taught that women were not as rational as men. From the beginning, the Bible offers up a negative sexual position. These ancient beliefs are still in play today in the twenty-first century. You can find evidence of the double standard applied to women throughout our culture.[23]

The Greeks continued the Egyptian sexual script by inheriting the system of having gods and goddesses who were sexually active. For the Greeks, spirituality and sexuality were integrated. Greek life was controlled by a system of gods and goddesses who participated in every dimension of life. They had a goddess of sexual intercourse by the name of Aphrodite who had a son through sexual intercourse that she named Eros.[24] Eros was the god of carnal love. When the deities we worship are sexual themselves, it frees us from feeling guilt, shame, or general negativity about our sexual practices. The Greeks could never do anything sexually that their gods were not doing. Being sexual was one of the ways the Greeks pleased the gods!

Nudity was also appreciated by the Greeks. The naked body was art! Since the gods themselves were nude, there was no shame or embarrassment about nudity. Greek art and sculpture demonstrates this point. Greek sporting events were done in the nude. The naked body was beautiful, sensual, and enjoyable to see. No shame was involved; no guilt felt and no fear of doing something wrong or evil if one looked at the naked body, were it real or a statue.

Finally, it should be noted that the Greeks had no homophobia. They had no word for homosexuality since it was their belief that human beings were all bisexual.²⁵ Prostitution was also included in their religious practices and had full acceptance throughout the social structure of the Greek culture. Spirituality and sexuality were integrated as one. They were in alignment. There was no guilt, no fear, no shame, and no embarrassment. Being sexual was pleasing to the gods. Aphrodite became their mother goddess of love.²⁶

The Romans inherited from the Greeks the system of sexual gods and goddesses who participated throughout their lives. Again, spirituality and sexuality were together in worship and ritual. Sexuality, as it was with the Egyptians and the Greeks, was a natural part of social and spiritual life. Nudity was appreciated as beautiful, fashionable, and wonderful to view. We know some of their sexual practices by the Latin roots to the words like "fellatio" and "cunnilingus," which relate to oral-genital stimulation. The male penis was considered a good luck charm. Archeologists have found penis amulets that were hung around the necks of children to protect them from evil. The penis amulet was not only a protector of children, but also of adults and even generals who went to war with the penis amulet attached to their chariots. The penis was believed to be the armor of the divine force. The penis was loved and appreciated by men, women, and children. It was displayed all over Rome in households and storefronts. Venus, who was the goddess of love, eventually became the divine mother goddess of Rome.²⁷

The Roman Empire was not without its troubles. Wars, slavery, taxes, economic corruption, and injustice caused much social unrest and conflict, to say the least. The Christian religion, which once had been persecuted and outlawed, was rising with popularity. As the Christian movement began to gain more and more power over time, the Emperor Constantine made Christianity the national religion of the Roman Empire. Constantine felt that by having a national religion Rome could be united. A united Rome was a stronger Rome. As time elapsed, the Roman Christian Church gained in power and control. By the fifth century, the Roman Catholic Church was in control not only of Rome, but also of the entire empire! From the fourth and fifth centuries until approximately the fifteenth century, the Roman Catholic Church controlled most of Western Civilization.²⁸ The system of gods and goddesses that was created by the Egyptians, Greeks, and Romans was replaced with a system of saints. Mary, the mother of Jesus, was named Mary, the Mother of God, often shortened to the Divine Mother. It is fascinating how the Egyptian goddess Isis became the Divine Mother; renamed by the Greeks as Aphrodite who became the Divine Mother; renamed by the Romans as Venus, who became the Divine Mother; and when the Christians gained rule of Rome, the followers of the Divine Mother goddess Venus were directed to follow Mary, the new Christian Divine Mother. As a Divine Mother is she not a Christian goddess?

How Sex Was Made Sinful

During the fourth and fifth centuries, Augustine, who eventually became a bishop and a saint, started writing about sexuality. Much of what he wrote would become the foundation of the sexual teachings for Western Civilization. His writings are still part of America's sexual script. In his preaching and writing, Augustine condemned sexuality as sinful and impure.[29] This was not a new idea to Christianity. Saint Paul was very fearful of sexuality and taught abstinence from having any sexual contact. He taught that a man should never touch a woman, but if he was too weak to control his desire, he should marry rather than sin.[30] Saint Augustine expanded on Saint Paul's teachings. Augustine saw sexuality as sinful. He taught that the sin of Adam and Eve in the book of Genesis was having sexual intercourse. He believed that sexual intercourse, even among married couples, was sinful. He taught that the sex act itself was sinful, even if a couple was married. He believed that sex should only be for procreation and not for any other purpose. He went further. Since babies are born through a sinful act (sexual intercourse), they are sinful at birth. Since God cannot look upon sin, babies can never see the face of God or go to heaven unless they are cleansed of their sin. Out of these teachings, the concept of original sin was developed. The sacrament of Baptism became the answer to this dilemma. If the baby goes through the rite of Baptism, it will then be cleansed of its parents' sin of having had sex, and will then be able to see God if it should die. Like Saint Paul, Saint Augustine stayed celibate. He promoted the concept of priestly celibacy. For Augustine, anyone having sex for anything other than to have children was sinning.[31]

Saint Thomas Aquinas, a thirteenteh-century Roman Catholic theologian, took the teachings of Saint Augustine and Saint Paul even further. He taught that any sexual behavior, whether one was married or not, was sinful. By that he meant that sexual thoughts, masturbation, stimulating oneself, foreplay, all were condemned as sinful. In fact, he taught that feeling any pleasure in sex at all was sinful! He believed that sex was only for procreation. Men should plant a seed and then get out of the garden! Aquinas taught that the greatest sin was having nongenital sex with oneself or someone else, including one's wife or husband. He believed there was only one legitimate sexual position: the male on top of the female. All other positions were condemned as being too arousing and therefore sinful. He believed that masturbation, homosexuality, and oral-genital contact were all, what he labeled as, "crimes against nature."[32] At one time, almost every state in the United States used this celibate thirteenth-century, Roman Catholic theologian's terminology in their legal sections on sex crimes. Many still do. Crimes against nature are usually considered oral and anal sex.

It is interesting to note that Aquinas also taught that rape, adultery, and incest were far less of a crime or sin than masturbation, homosexuality, or oral and anal sex. His reasoning was that at least in rape, adultery, and incest one could produce a baby, which would partly legitimize the sex-for-reproduction doctrine. The punishments and penances for masturbation were greater than for rape.[33] If we examine the Church's sexual script during the Middle Ages, it is clear that the restrictive teachings of the first-century Christians were adopted and reinforced in the Middle Ages. The rules on sexuality were made restrictive and oppressive.[34] Even now in the twenty-first century, America's sexual script is officially abstinence until marriage. The United States government invests over two hundred million dollars a year from our taxes to support the teaching of abstinence until marriage. Masturbation is still a mortal sin by the official doctrine of the Roman Catholic Church. Over sixty million Catholics in the United States are still taught that the use of birth control is sinful. The use of birth control is sinful because sex should only be for procreation.[35] Oral and anal sex are considered sinful, and the teaching of sex in marriage only for procreation is the only legitimate sex.

Recently, a student in one of my human sexuality classes asked her priest if it was true that sex was only for procreation. He said, "No, that is not true. You can have sex in marriage to strengthen your relationship." She then asked him if that was so, could she and her husband use birth control. He said, "No, because if you used birth control, you might prevent God from performing a miracle in giving you a baby. You'd be preventing God from bringing a life into the world!" Although an interesting rationalization, the priest did not remember official Church doctrine, which has not changed since the Middle Ages: sex is only for procreation.

How the Negative Sexual Script Was Made into Law

Both Protestant and Catholic Christianity hold to the belief that sex should only be in marriage. Masturbation is sinful because it involves lust. Homosexuality is sinful because the Bible condemns it. Oral-genital contact is sinful because the only rightful sex is a penis in the vagina. Again, this is validating the sex-for-reproduction-only doctrine. If you put the penis anywhere else, it becomes a "crime against nature."

When we examine the laws concerning sexual practices in the United States, we can see how the Christian sexual script of the first century has been voted into law. Places where oral sex has been made illegal include: Alabama, Arizona, Florida, Idaho, Kansas, Louisiana, Massachusetts, Minnesota, Mississippi, Georgia, Oklahoma, Oregon, Rhode Island, Utah, Virginia, and Washington DC.[36]

Having sex outside of marriage is illegal in Idaho, Georgia, Massachusetts, Rhode Island, Virginia, North Carolina, South Carolina, and Mississippi.[37]

Adultery is a crime in Wisconsin, Michigan, Minnesota, Idaho, Nevada, California, Colorado, Utah, Illinois, Tennessee, Georgia, Florida, New York, West Virginia, Massachusetts, New Hampshire, Rhode Island, Maryland, Virginia, North Carolina, South Carolina, Alabama, Mississippi, and Nebraska.[38]

Heterosexual anal sex is against the law, even for married couples, in the following states: Idaho, Wyoming, Oregon, Nevada, Minnesota, Missouri, Louisiana, Utah, Mississippi, Alabama, Florida, Georgia, North Carolina, South Carolina, Washington DC, Rhode Island, and Massachusetts.[39]

On June 23, 2003, in a six-to-three decision, the United States Supreme Court ruled that sodomy laws (classified as "Crimes against Nature"), which include both oral and anal sex, are unconstitutional.[40] Actually, all these laws are unconstitutional, but most of these states retain them as legal and still occasionally enforce them. In 1971, Idaho became the first state to repeal its sodomy law, but outrage from the Mormon and Catholic churches forced the reinstatement of the entire old code with the felony sodomy law. Idaho became the first state to reinstate a repealed sodomy law.[41] It is interesting to note that three Supreme Court justices ruled against making these laws unconstitutional.

The first-century Christian sexual script is still being supported today by the governing bodies of both our federal and state representatives. At last count, thirty-three of our fifty states required mandatory teaching of abstinence until marriage in our schools.[42] Often the authorities and institutions that support abstinence are also against oral-genital contact, anal sex, comprehensive sex education, contraception, and the morning-after pill. The providing and use of condoms is still controversial; sex education is censored, controlled, and limited. Homosexuality is condemned. Those who hold these views are often against women's rights and the feminist position.

When we study the sources of these negative sexual teachings that we have in America, we cannot ignore politics, religion, and the interpretation of the Bible by the Christian Church. Christianity, more than any other religion in America, has had the greatest negative influence on our understanding of sexuality and our feelings about sexual practices. This is not because Christianity is more negative than other religions. It is that Christianity is the religion that gained control of Western Civilization and instituted its beliefs into our culture.[43] The Puritans, Protestants, and Catholics transported Christianity to America. Christianity became the dominant religion in America. We need to take a fresh look at what the Bible teaches about sex and what Jesus taught about sex. This will enhance our understanding of our culture's sexual legacy and how it has had a dark effect on our sexuality.

After the fifteenth century, with the advent of modern science, the Church was very threatened to have many of its beliefs and assumptions not only challenged but also proven wrong. Galileo was arrested by the Church. When he died, he was still under house arrest. He had to stop teaching that the earth was not the center of the universe in order to prevent his own execution.[44]

The negative sexual teachings in our culture condemn masturbation and condom use. In addition, sexual information is censored and distorted. The withholding of honest, accurate, and comprehensive sex education contributes to the fear, guilt, shame, and ignorance that so many people have with their sexuality. Many people, therefore, are vulnerable to the misinformation found in the negative scripting so prevalent in this culture. Healthy, comprehensive sex education is a primary antidote to the negative sexual teachings. The influences of Saints Paul, Augustine, and Aquinas need urgently to be ameliorated at this time in our history. We need to move beyond the Middle Ages!

A contemporary example of comprehensive sex education and its positive effects is the Netherlands. The Dutch people do not teach abstinence. They believe that when children become old enough to have sex, they most likely will. They prepare young people for sex by teaching them responsibility rather than abstinence. The government provides free contraception and free abortion. Therefore, they report the lowest teen pregnancy rate per capita, and the lowest abortion rate per capita of any other country in the industrialized world.[45]

Today, the adherence to the negative sexual scripting continues to reverberate in our culture. There is a contradiction between our sexual feelings and needs, and how we have been sexually scripted. The hypocrisy of publicly endorsing one behavior and privately practicing its opposite is rampant. It has most recently been evidenced by many of our politicians, Protestant clergy, and Catholic priests. Some practice homosexuality in private but take strong stands against gay rights in public. Some also profess to be Christian moralists in public, yet in their private lives they have affairs. Some vote and campaign for pro-life, while secretly securing abortions for their mistresses. Then there are those priests who take vows of celibacy but are privately sexually active[46] and the priests who act as strong spiritual moralists while secretly committing criminal, unethical, abusive acts against children. The church tells us to confess our sins, while it does all it can to hide and cover up its own sin. It appears that the beliefs that have been made up about sexuality are contrary to the nature of human beings.

It is noteworthy how positive the sexual scripts of Egypt, Greece, and Rome were before the advent of Christianity, and how negative and fearful the sexual script became when Christianity came into control in Western culture. In 1517, when Martin Luther presented his ninety-five complaints regarding the corruption and hypocrisy of the Church, he began the Protestant Reformation. Martin Luther saw that the leaders of the upper administration of the Church preached one message in public and practiced its opposite in private. The hypocrisy of publicly endorsing and acting celebate, while privately having sexual encounters, became intolerable to Luther. He felt that if celibacy did not work, and he could see that it did not, then the Church should give it up. When Luther left, he married a nun and taught the importance of the clergy being married. He also taught that a husband and wife could have sex for pleasure and enjoyment, not just for procreation.[47] He was very influential in starting a movement in history toward a more positive view of sexuality. A more positive view of sexuality became allowable with the breaking of the power of the Church to control both thought and sexual practices. The coming of the Renaissance, the Age of Reason, which questioned much of what the Church was teaching, and the beginning of modern science to some extent liberated sexuality from the restrictive and repressive control of the Protestant and Catholic Churches. I am aware that I am making a much-generalized statement since social changes and revolutions involve very complex processes and multiple influences and conditions. I am making a broad overview to move us through history to the Victorian period.

The Victorian Negative Sexual Script

To further elucidate our current sexual attitudes and struggle for healthy sexuality it is important to understand the influence of the Victorian era. Dubbed a period of "moral revival," it dates from 1839 when Queen Victoria assumed the English throne until 1901. Victorianism was a countermovement in reaction to the sexual freedom and liberation of the sixteenth and seventeenth centuries. It was a movement to return to a stricter, more conservative, and repressive sexual script. The teachings of the Victorian era were predominant until 1920, but many of the sexual beliefs of that period had an influence into the 1950s in America. Some examples of this influence is the scripting in the 1950s that all women should be virgins until they get married and masturbation is sinful, unhealthy, and should not be done; also, the censoring and withholding of comprehensive sex information, and the belief that no one should view or read anything that might be arousing.

Victorian thinking suggested that men had a pathological desire for sex; that men were obsessed and addicted to a sexual passion unknown to women. It was believed that a well-adjusted, healthy woman had no desire for sex. During this period, Dr. William Acton, MD, wrote a very popular book on sex that was the most widely read book of the second half of the nineteenth century. It was entitled *The Functions and Disorders of the Reproductive Organs*. In his writings, Acton claimed that, "the majority of women have no sexual feeling of any kind. Love of home, children, and domestic duties are the only passions they feel."[48] Since women have no sexual desire, according to him, they would have to try not to make things more difficult for men by tempting them in any way.

Women were taught to feel responsible for male morality. Therefore, women were to dress in a way that would hide their bodies from men.

Victorian fashion for females included large hoop skirts with layer after layer of undergarments, which went to the floor to hide their buttocks and their legs. Blouses were to cover all flesh from the wrist up, and necklines were to be buttoned up to their chin. Men and women were to be segregated from each other in social and public life. Sex segregation was socially enforced. There was a ban on all books judged as obscene and pornographic. Any books with erotic content were burned and destroyed. Even many of the classics written by Shakespeare, Milton, and Dante were removed from the public and burned.[49]

Medicine's Contribution to the Negative Sexual Script

Modern medicine was just beginning to develop. Medicine, in its ignorance, taught that sex, and especially orgasm, was dangerous to your health. Medical doctors taught that masturbation would make you insane and cause you to become paralyzed or blind. All of the books written as medical advisors listed all the symptoms of illnesses caused by masturbation and sexual intercourse. Sexuality became couched in fear and paranoia. Special wire cages were made to lock around the genitals of children to keep them from arousing themselves when in bed at night. Nude statutes in parks and museums were covered, and even animals had to wear a covering over their genitals.

It was taught that sex was more than just a sin against God; it was also unhealthy.[50] Keeping all knowledge of sexuality from adults and children so that they were completely ignorant about sex was one of the most important goals of the Victorian revolution. The Victorian period was an attempt to return to the earlier restrictive and repressed time in history.

The Movement toward a More Positive Sexual Script

The countermovement to this period was the Roaring Twenties. In the 1920s, women revolted. They organized to get their voting rights, their rights to contraception, and their right to be sexual. They changed women's fashion by going from a hooped skirt to a miniskirt and from a buttoned-up blouse to a plunging neckline. They danced the Charleston. They won the right to vote, and they developed a new interest in being sexual.[51] The pendulum was swinging back to the left when the Great Depression of 1929 reversed the swing back to conservatism.

The Movement to Return to a More Negative Sexual Script

With the start of World War II, people became worried and frightened. A new Christian revival began emphasizing the traditional sexual script of abstinence until marriage, the evils and sin of masturbation, sex for procreation, restricted access to contraception, and no comprehensive sex education. The goal was to keep as much information as possible about sex out of the reach of people so that they would not sin. It was important to censor anything sexual. Teaching ignorance was the menu of the day. It was important to warn everyone about the sin of lust and God's wrath and his hell! When World War II ended and men came home from the war, the government emphasized the importance of procreation, marriage, and having a family. Women were to give the men their jobs back and become homemakers. Women were to marry, have babies, and take care of the home and their husbands.[52]

The Sexual Revolution for a More Positive Sexual Script

The result of years of "teaching ignorance" and censoring all sexual information from the public left Americans starved for sexual information. In the 1950s, more than 85 percent of American married women were not able to experience orgasm. Most of them had never had one, and they did not know how to have an orgasm.[53] Americans were sexually ignorant. Sexual information had been censured, and the social mores taught that to think about or talk about sex was sinful. People feared the subject; they avoided any discussion of sex. The subject had become shameful and embarrassing. To mention anything about sexuality or even sexual states, like menstruation, pregnancy, or menopause, could cause instant condemnation and social rejection.

In 1948, biologist Alfred Kinsey, PhD, from Harvard published his research survey on "Sexual Behavior in the Human Male." It created a storm of protests and anger. The moral authorities and institutions were outraged at Kinsey and his survey. In 1953, Kinsey published "Sexual Behavior in the Human Female." His surveys became controversial, to say the least. Kinsey was seen as dangerous to society. He was fired from his professorship position at the University of Illinois. His research grants were cancelled, and his survey was condemned by most of the churches, politicians, and "righteous citizens." Kinsey had completed the first survey of the sexual practices in American.[54] What he found revealed a real hypocrisy in American society. In public, everyone appeared to be practicing what all the clergy were preaching, but in private, there was a surprising rate of masturbation, sexual infidelity, and sex before marriage. His findings opened up controversy about what was sexually right or wrong. What was sexually normal? American's were talking about sex. Sexual debate broke out all over the country.

In 1953, a twenty-six-year-old writer saw America's need for sexual liberation from the negative, restrictive, distorted, and false sexual script that had once again become the standard for Americans. His name was Hugh Hefner, and he published the first issue of *Playboy Magazine* with Marilyn Monroe nude in the centerfold. Only a small percentage of *Playboy* depicted nude pictures of females; the rest included scholarly articles on sexuality, and advertising. Although the "monster moralists" were outraged, the magazine sold by the thousands.[55] America was desperate for sexual information that was honest, accurate, and uncensored. Both Kinsey's and Hefner's work helped initiate a sexual revolution and a sex industry. They created a new interest in sexuality. American society was torn between those who welcomed sexual openness and information, and those who feared it would destroy the Christian moral fiber of the country.

The 1960s Movement for Positive Sexuality

With the beginning of the 1960s, in response to the negative sexual script, the need for a social and sexual revolution became apparent. The moral pendulum was swinging to the left. Traditional sexual values simply did not work for the majority of Americans. It was time for change, and the change came. The FDA approved the birth control pill. There were practically no sexually transmitted diseases that were life threatening. The information from Kinsey and *Playboy Magazine* helped create a voracious interest in everything sexual. There was a new challenge to free up the rigid gender roles and change the social mores that the past generation had established. The frustration with the hypocrisy and the sexual repression in society inspired a revolt to change America's negative sexual script. A social movement to explore and experiment provided a foundation for new sexual research. The work of Masters and Johnson used a method never done before. They used direct observation of couples actually having sex in the collection of their data.[56]

Historic Swings of the Positive/Negative Scripting

In reviewing this brief history of sexuality, we need to frame sexuality and morality as a process in which sexual scripts and moral beliefs are dynamic, not static. Beginning with the Egyptians, Greeks, and early Romans, the sexual script was positive. With the advent of Christian power and control of Western Civilization, we moved to a negative, fearful, restrictive sexual script. With the Reformation, the Renaissance, the Age of Reason, and the advent of modern science, we had a swing back to a more positive and free sexual script, but with the counterreaction, which was the Victorian movement, the script was made negative again. The counterreaction to the Victorian movement was the newfound freedom of the Roaring Twenties. The Great Depression and World War II gave the traditional, Christian, negative script new life through the 1950s. The changes of the 1960s swung the moral pendulum back to a more positive and informed sexual script.

The Beginning of the Neo-Victorian Negative Script

With the election of President Ronald Reagan in 1982, a movement was initiated to return to a more fearful, negative, repressive, and restrictive sexual script in American culture. Sexual freedom and information was under attack. Homosexuality was falsely blamed for the AIDS virus. A new move against gay rights, free choice about abortion, and comprehensive sex education in our schools became important social issues. A new effort to teach abstinence from having sex until marriage and a strong movement against pornography was inspired by President Reagan. He commissioned Attorney General Edwin Meese to form a committee to study the negative effects of pornography.[57] With the election of President George W. Bush, it seemed that America was again moving toward a Neo-Victorian sexual script.[58]

Certainly social and historical revolutions and movements are complex and multi-faceted, both in etiology and in outcome. Admittedly, I have taken the liberty to generalize the historical changes that have taken place in history. The point here is that every action inspires a reaction. Sexual beliefs seem to move from being more permissive to being more restrictive to being more permissive, etc. For our purposes, this brief history has been an attempt to simply enhance our understanding of how our current sexual teachings in America evolved over time and history. It is one perspective. It is a statement to make the reader aware that sexuality has never actually been fixed in history. Sexual beliefs and practices are not static, but dynamic. In Western culture, and in particular American culture, sexual teachings have cycled from a more restrictive to a less restrictive to a more restrictive to a less restrictive scripting.

There seems to always be a running debate about what is morally right concerning sexuality. Is it wrong to have sex outside of marriage, use birth control, take a morning-after pill, masturbate, watch erotic movies, swim nude, or "do it" on the first date? Are oral sex and anal sex okay? How about all those different sexual positions? Can you have sex without love? Is it okay to have sex just for the tension release? Mate swap? Threesomes? Have sex in front of another couple? As you think about these questions, what is the rationale for your answer? What determines right and wrong?

Chapter Two:

The Bible, Lust, and Sexuality

Jim is a solid family man with two young children and a devoted wife. He is a fundamentalist Christian who prides himself in reading the Bible every day. He has a strong faith and clarity about what he believes. He is a sincere man who cares about people. He strives to live a godly life following what he believes the Bible teaches. His Bible is his inspiration for his faith. The primary meaning in Jim's life is to live by the word of God as he interprets it from the Bible. He says he has no doubts that only through Jesus Christ can anyone be saved and get to heaven.

Next door to Jim live Ted and Mel. Ted and Mel are homosexual in their orientation. They have lived together for fifteen years. They feel a deep love for each other and seem to get along very well. They are affectionate and devoted. They are out of the closet and make no apology for being gay. Both of them have a strong conviction that they were born with their sexual orientation. They just bought the house next door to Jim and moved into the neighborhood a week ago.

Ted was sitting on his front steps when Jim came over to introduce himself. With a welcoming handshake, Jim informed Ted that he was a Christian, and he wanted to know if Ted knew the Lord Jesus Christ. Ted told him right up front that he was a gay man but not a Christian. When Jim started to quote bible verses at Ted, he had no idea that Ted knew some things about the Bible that Jim had never discovered. In response to Jim telling him that the Bible is the very word of God and that it teaches that homosexuality is an abomination, Ted took Jim's Bible from his hand and started reading some verses to him. Ted pointed out to Jim that some of the verses he read could not be the word of God. Ted also pointed out that Jim was applying some verses but not others.

It is obvious that the Bible can be comforting and inspirational to many believers. However, people often do not examine what they are told. Many believers are taught never to question its authority. An examination of the Bible's teachings about sexuality will demonstrate the lack of helpful information and the large volume of negativity about sexuality and women.

Using the Bible to Control Our Thinking and Our Sexuality

The church claims that the Bible is the word of God. It believes that it is God's revelation to the world. However, there are some serious problems with that concept. I will not discuss all the scholarly work that has uncovered serious textual, as well as conceptual, problems of the Bible. I do want to address some more obvious issues of scripture. Some scriptures reflect what appears to be ancient tribal teaching. Some scriptures sound more like the word of men, not that of an intelligent god. The real question is what authority should Bible scripture have over our sexual lives? Let us look at some examples of scripture that support what Ted was trying to show Jim.

From the Old Testament:

Leviticus 18:22[59]
You shall not lie with a man as with a woman.
    This verse is constantly quoted by those homophobic people who are against gay rights, gay marriage, and gay anything. Homosexuality is clearly wrong according to this Bible verse. Jim had this verse memorized and had no trouble quoting it to Ted.

Leviticus 19:26–28[60]
You shall not eat any flesh with blood in it … you shall not make any cuttings in your flesh … or tattoo any marks upon you: I am the Lord.
    I do not think the beef industry would like us to apply this verse as the truth of God. Would this not also apply to all the people who have tattoos? Where is the church's outcry about meat and tattoos? Those church potlucks should all be vegetarian. This verse is very clear on what God wants; let's apply it.

Exodus 35:1–3[61]
These are the things, which the Lord commanded you to do. Six days shall work be done, but on the seventh day you shall have a holy Sabbath of solemn rest to the Lord: whoever does any work on it shall be put to death; you shall kindle no fire in all your habitations on the Sabbath day.

It is also obvious what the Lord wants here. Let us put to death everyone who works on Saturdays! We can do that at the same time we are executing homosexuals.

Leviticus 20:10–13[62]
If a man commits adultery with the wife of his neighbor, both the adulterer and the adulteress shall be put to death. If a man lies with his father's wife, both of them shall be put to death. If a man lies with his daughter-in-law, both of them shall be put to death; if a man lies with a male, as with a woman, they should be put to death.

Here it is again. The word of God says to kill adulterers and homosexuals, at least the male ones! So if we are going to apply the word of God to our lives, why just be selective of gays?

Leviticus 25:44–46[63]
As for your male and female slaves whom you may have: you may buy male and female slaves from among the nations that are round about you. You may also buy from among the strangers who sojourn with you and their families that are with you.

Did you know that the Bible supports slavery? If this is the word of God, then the Confederacy of the southern states did have God on their side in 1860 and 1861!

Deuteronomy 21:18–21[64]
If a man has a stubborn and rebellious son who will not obey the voice of his father or the voice of his mother, and who, when they have chastened him, will not heed them, then his father and mother shall take hold of him and bring him out to the elders of the city, to the gate of the city. In addition, they shall say to the elders of the city, "this son of ours is stubborn and rebellious; he will not obey our voice; he is a glutton and a drunkard." Then the men of this city shall stone him to death with stones; so, you shall put away the evil from among you.

Would you agree that this is good advice for how to handle an incorrigible teenager? Does an intelligent God think this way? If it is the word of God, why not apply it toward teenagers as we apply Leviticus 18:22 toward gays? Let us be consistent.

Here are a few more verses from the Bible to guide you on child rearing and discipline:

Proverbs 13:24[65]
He who spares the rod hates his son, but he who loves him is diligent to discipline him.
Proverbs 22:15[66]
Folly is bound up in the heart of a child, but the rod of discipline drives it far from him.
Proverbs 23:13–14[67]
Do not withhold discipline from a child; if you beat him with a rod, he will not die. If you beat him with a rod, you will save his life from Sheol.

Now we know where "spare the rod and spoil the child" came from. Does this mean that the Bible, the word of God, supports child abuse?

Leviticus 20:27[68]
A man or a woman who is a medium (a psychic) or a wizard shall be put to death; they shall be stoned with stones.
Deuteronomy 22:5[69]
A woman shall not wear anything that pertains to a man, nor shall a man put on a woman's garment; for whoever does these things, it is an abomination to the Lord your God.

Again, we have the Bible telling us to kill psychic people. We all know them. These include palm readers, tarot card interpreters, and psychic readers. In addition, what about women wearing men's clothing such as suits, pants, and shoes? One response to these Biblical verses is that they are from the Old Testament, which is the Old Covenant we had with God. These verses no longer apply because Jesus Christ brought about a New Covenant with God. If that is so, then why do so many Christians keep quoting Leviticus 18:22 against homosexuality? If these verses are the word of God, does that mean that God changed His mind when He made the New Covenant? Moreover, if these verses are not the word of God, but rather the tribal laws of ancient Israel, then why have them? We can toss out the Old Testament then, because it is the outdated word of God!

Let us turn to the New Testament, which is supposed to be the New Covenant we have with God. It is also believed to be the Word of God.

Colossians 3:22[70]
Slaves, obey in everything those who are your earthly masters.
Ephesians 6:5–7[71]
Slaves, be obedient to those who are your earthly masters, with fear and trembling … rendering service with a good will as to the lord.

Again, both the Old Testament and the New Testament support slavery. No wonder the Confederate southern states felt so righteous about being allowed to keep their slaves!

1 Corinthians 7:1–2[72]
It is well for a man not to touch a woman, but because of the temptation to immorality, each man should have his own wife and each woman her own husband.
1 Corinthians 7:8–9[73]
To the unmarried and widows I say that it is well for them to remain single as I do. However, if they cannot exercise self-control, they should marry. For it is better to marry than to be aflame with passion.

What do these passages say about women? Stay away from them and marry them only as sexual recipients? What do these passages say about marriage? That marriage is a last resort for people who cannot manage celibacy and their sexual passions? Clearly these passages support abstinence from sex, unless one is married, but they certainly do not make marriage honorable.

1 Timothy 2:11–14[74]
Let a woman learn in silence with all submissiveness. I permit no woman to teach or to have authority over men: she is to keep silent. For Adam was formed first, then Eve: And Adam was not deceived, but the woman was deceived and became the transgressor.
Colossians 3:18[75]
Wives be subject to your husbands, as is fitting in the Lord.
1 Corinthians 14:33–35[76]
As in all the churches of the saints, the women should keep silence in the churches. For they are not permitted to speak, but should be subordinate as even the law says. If there is anything they desire to know, let them ask their husbands at home. For it is shameful for a woman to speak in church.

Is this the word of God or Saint Paul's own bias about women? Alternatively, is this just first-century culture? These scriptures imply a distrust of women who are believed to be morally weak; they are the "transgressors." There are other verses emphasizing that men should love their wives, but that does not change the status of women as somehow less than that of a man. The men have the right to speak in church, but the women do not? Men can have authority over women, but women cannot have authority over men? Yes, the Bible says for men to love their wives, but they do not have to be submissive to their wives as women have to be submissive to their husbands. Why do women have to submit? Because men are a little better than women are? A little smarter than women? Are they more rational than women are? Are men stronger morally than women? Is this double standard the inspired word of God, or do these verses really represent Saint Paul reinforcing the cultural view on women during his lifetime?

So many Christians, including ministers and priests, will distort scripture to support their own biased opinion. An example is the use of Leviticus 18:22 to support their own homophobia. Is God homophobic? Does God feel that women are lesser humans than males? What does God feel about sexuality? The truth is that the Bible really teaches almost nothing about sexuality. We could sum up most of the biblical information on sex in two sentences: do not commit adultery, and abstain from sex until marriage. There is not much education in that information. What did Jesus teach about sexuality? Jesus taught just about nothing at all. He did not seem to be interested in the subject. He never said anything about abortion or birth control. He did not directly address the subject of abstinence from sex until marriage. He never mentioned the issue of masturbation. He did not address the issue of oral or anal sex. In fact, unlike His churches today, He was not obsessed with sexual issues at all. He did seem to spend a lot of his ministry addressing hypocrisy, dishonesty, and the plight of the poor.

There is one passage in which Jesus makes a reference to lust, but this passage has been corrupted by both the Catholic and the Protestant churches for centuries. Again, this passage has been distorted to support a sexual bias, which creates guilt about being a sexual person. Because this passage, supposedly spoken by Jesus, gets to the core of our libido, it gives the church incredible power to make us feel guilty about our normal and natural state of being a sexual person. Guilt and fear increase church membership and income. Let us take a new look at this passage. It is sometimes referred to as the lust passage, but Jesus was not really talking about sex in this passage. It is found in Matthew, Chapter 5, starting with verse 27. Jesus is giving one of His sermons, and He is quoted as saying the following: "You have heard that it was said, 'you shall not commit adultery'. But I say to you that everyone who looks at a woman lustfully has already committed adultery with her in his heart."[77]

Pope John Paul II said in a sermon delivered in Saint Peter's Square and again in Philadelphia on October 8, 1980, that "adultery in the heart is committed not only because a man looks in a certain way at a woman who is not his wife … but precisely because he is looking at a woman that way. Even if he were to look that way at his wife, he could be committing adultery."[78] The Pope suggests that being turned on by our wife's body or our husband's is potentially sinful. Has he never figured it out that without lust there can be no erections? No males can perform without sexual desire. The Pope's statement is worse than just hairsplitting; it is just plain ludicrous.

It is unfortunate that a traditional belief cannot be changed. The traditional interpretation of both the Protestant Church and the Roman Catholic Church was that Jesus was condemning lust as sinful; that anyone who ever has a sexual fantasy about anyone other than his wife or her husband is guilty of sinning. Specifically, that person is then guilty of committing adultery in his or her heart. That makes fantasy no different from real life!

The Power of Lust as a Negative Concept

In 1976, President Jimmy Carter agreed to give an interview to *Playboy Magazine*. The interview was going along well, until he was asked if he was a Christian. He said he was. Then the interviewer asked him if he ever lusted after other women. Carter then said, "I try not to commit a deliberate sin. I recognize that I am going to do it anyhow because I am human, and I am tempted, and Christ set some impossible standards for us … I've looked on a lot of women with lust. I have committed adultery in my heart many times. This is something that God recognizes that I would do, and I have done it and God forgives me for it."[79] Why didn't Jimmy follow the rest of the teaching? The next verse says, "if your eye causes you to sin, pluck it out; it is better to be blind than to burn in Hell." There is nothing in this "lust passage" that says God will forgive you. The next verse does tell you what God expects you to do.

Matthew 5:27–30[80]
You have heard that it was said, 'you shall not commit adultery', But I say to you that every one who looks at a woman lustfully has already committed

adultery with her in his heart. If your right eye causes you to sin, pluck it out and throw it away; It is better that you lose one of your members than that your whole body be thrown into hell. And if your right hand causes you to sin, cut it off and throw it away; it is better that you lose one of your members than that your whole body go into hell.

Poor Jimmy Carter! He was hoodwinked by the negative sexual scripting, promoted by a combination of all the individuals, authorities, and institutions that have supported and perpetuated a negative sexual view. The negative sexual writings are designed to make us feel guilty, fearful, and ashamed about our sexuality. Why should we feel guilty about what is a natural part of our biology? The biological desire to mate is a natural part of our physiology and being. If we put this lust verse in context with what is before and what comes after in the text, it becomes obvious that Jesus was not talking about sex in this passage. Now look at the verse that comes before the lust verse.

Matthew 5:21–22[81]
You have heard that it was said to the men of old, 'you shall not kill; and whoever kills shall be liable to judgment.' But I say to you that every one who is angry with his brother shall be liable to judgment; Whoever insults his brother shall be liable to judgment; whoever insults his brother shall be liable to the council, and whoever says, 'You fool!' Shall be liable to the hell of fire.

Essentially, Jesus is saying that to get angry is no different from killing. "You shall not kill," but even if we just get angry with someone, it is the same as killing him or her. To get angry brings the same punishment as killing someone. When we get angry with someone, we have committed murder in our hearts. Look at Matthew 5:20. Jesus is speaking about the self-righteousness of the religious leaders, the Scribes and Pharisees. They were the religious leaders during the time of Jesus. Jesus taught that they wore a mask of righteousness and prided themselves in how good they believed they were in the eyes of God. They prided themselves in believing that they kept all of the Jewish Ten Commandments of Moses. They had never killed anyone; they had not ever committed adultery. This they felt made them holy men. They felt special in the eyes of God. They kept all of God's rules. They also believed they knew everything about God; they had all the answers to any question that might be asked about God.

Jesus exposes the fact that they are all hypocrites; He called them "whitewashed tombs."[82] Jesus knew the human condition. He knew that no human could ever really be holy. He knew that no human could ever be righteous. When we combine all these passages into their context, we can see the obvious: it is humanly impossible not to ever get angry; it is humanly impossible to see women and not have sexual thoughts and fantasies. Jesus is teaching that it is as impossible to never get angry or look lustfully at a woman as it would be for you to be able to just pluck out your eye or cut off your arm. Let us review: if you get angry with someone, you have murdered them in your heart; if you have sexual thoughts about someone, you have had sex with them and committed adultery in your heart; and if you were really able to be holy as a human being, you would have to remove your humanity from yourself. Jimmy Carter should have plucked out his eye so that he could stop lusting after women! As humans, we cannot refrain from getting angry or feeling sexual desire and attraction to someone. We can never rid ourselves of our humanity, and therefore we can never be holy.

If you think about it, Jesus is really "pulling our leg" in this teaching. He is showing his sense of humor. How could anyone cut off their arm or pluck out their eye? No one can do that. Jesus is saying you cannot be holy either. When it comes to humans being righteous and holy, Jesus set the bar where it is humanly impossible for anyone to attain such purity. It is a given that we will have anger and we will have lust. Jesus is not talking about sex; he is talking about what real godliness is. It is something humans really cannot attain. Humans cannot become anything like God. Our humanity disqualifies us from ever being holy. Jesus was attacking the self-righteousness and legalism of the Scribes and Pharisees, but he was not talking about sex. Practicing all that religious ritual and liturgy might make you feel good, but it does not make you holy in the eyes of God. Following all the commandments and other rules might give you a sense of security, but it does not make you righteous in the eyes of God. In this passage, Jesus is teaching that true righteousness is something no human being can attain, but he is also confirming that it is normal and natural for humans to have anger and lust. He was not teaching that lust or anger is sinful. He was teaching that lust and anger were common experiences of all men. Anger and lust are normal human qualities. Jesus was not condemning anger or lust. He was teaching that they are a part of our humanity. It is our humanity that keeps us from being able to be truly holy. For a person to have lust is perceived by Jesus as normal.

Why have the churches taken the lust verse out of its context? Because it serves their purpose to make people feel guilty and fearful about their sexuality. It fills the churches and the offering plates; it makes people feel the need to be saved; it creates the need for confession and absolution; and it keeps the churches wealthy and powerful. The guilt and fear the church has scripted not only helps the churches to profit, but it also helps sexual addiction rehabilitation groups, where corporate interests profit off the fear, guilt, and shame that the negative sexual script creates.

Lust, a Part of Our Natural Humanity

Any sexually healthy person, male or female, is going to feel sexual desire. There will be times when it will be very intense. That is the definition of lust: intense sexual desire that results in a deep erotic state, as when we feel horny or erotic. Without lust, there will not be erections of the penis or the clitoris. We are all biologically hardwired to have strong and intense sexual feeling. It is the design of nature or, if you prefer, it is the design of God. All living things are designed to procreate. Intense sexual feelings, or lust, are part of the procreation design. Without lust, there would be sexual dysfunction. There would be no orgasms or babies. Too often, religion takes what is natural and condemns it as unnatural; it takes what is unnatural and teaches it as natural. Two examples are the false teachings of the lust verse and the teaching of celibacy. The condemnation of lust justifies not seeing nudity or reading anything that might sexually arouse someone. Even among married couples, some foreplay could be experienced as sinful. The church's position on lust can justify censorship of anything sexual, even honest and accurate information about sexuality.

The Weakness of the Bible as a Moral Authority

The Bible is not a good text for the subject of human sexuality or gender studies. As you may recall, many of the teachings in the Bible are very negative about women, and other teachings are outdated. If God did send a revelation into the world, it would have to enter time and place within a culture. That explains why the Old Testament was first written in Hebrew and not English. Most of the New Testament manuscripts are written in Greek, not English. They are written in these languages because of the time in which the revelation entered the world, as well as the place it entered. Does it not stand to reason that any revelation that enters culture is going to have some of the cultural beliefs and practices reflective of that culture? That is why we should not do what everyone so often does, including clergymen: extract a verse that supports our own personal biases or prejudices and quote it with authority. Out of context we can find a verse to support almost anything. So let us say that not everything in the Bible that is reflective of the culture of its time is revelation, but rather, ancient beliefs and practices of a past culture. Examples would be the Bible's support of slavery, its oppression of women, its messages of abuse toward children, or its prescription to stone people to death for any disobedience against the law. These abuses are not revelations, but ancient culture and tribal customs. We have to discriminate between spiritual revelation that is universal for all ages and what is limited to time and place, such as the first-century culture. A spiritual truth or revelation would be something applicable to every age, a truth that has universal application to life. So, what might be a spiritual truth? One example might be the verse, "Love your neighbor as you love yourself."[83]

We need to recognize that the Bible is not an authority on sex. In order to become more accepting of our erotic dimension, we must be able to see the distortion and misinformation that is often backed up with Bible verses and corrupted interpretations of scripture. The people who fear erotica often use the Bible as an authority to support their discomfort with sex. Jesus had little to say about sex. Most of the Bible's teachings reflect the culture of the time in which it was written. If you can recognize this, then you can be free to determine what is sexually right or wrong for yourself. You should be the authority on your sexuality.

Chapter Three:

Making Erotica Instead of Making Love

The Importance of Erotic Language

Another product we have inherited from negative sexual scripting is the camouflaging and shrouding of sexual language. We have technical and clinical language for sexual terminology like penis, vagina, breast, intercourse, and testicles, but when we are talking personally and intimately with friends or with a partner, we often use synonyms that are suggestive of sexual anatomy and sexual states. For penis, we might say "cock," or "dick." For vagina, we might say "pussy" or "cunt." For breasts, we might say "boobs," and for intercourse, we might say "screw" or "fuck" or "make love." For testicles, we might say "nuts" or "balls." When it comes to having sex with someone, use of the formal technical language is not helpful. It is not helpful because it does not communicate erotic feeling, which is what sex should primarily be about. So, the street language that has been made up so that we can talk in a language that communicates erotic feeling becomes very important in sexual communication. More importantly, the use of this erotic language can stimulate arousal of more intense sexual passion.

In the years that I have been a licensed marriage counselor, I have counseled two cases that illustrate the point. In one case, the presenting problem was that the wife could not reach an orgasm while having sex with her husband unless he would talk "dirty talk" while they were having intercourse. In this case, the wife married a devout Catholic man who felt that to use that street language on his wife was a sin. For him it was disrespectful. He felt that one should never talk like that to a woman who is his wife and whom he loves. She would get upset with him if he didn't, and he would get upset with her for insisting on it when she knew it was sinful for him. She would often get him intoxicated before they had sex, and then he would use the dirty language and she would be able to have an orgasm. The next morning, however, he would be angry with her for manipulating him to do it.

In the second case, it was just the opposite. The husband liked to talk dirty talk to his wife while having foreplay and during intercourse. His wife felt that such language would be used when addressing a whore, but not with someone you loved and respected.

The Madonna-Whore Complex

This previous case illustrates some of the characteristics of the popular "Madonna-whore complex." The contrast between Eve and Mary, the Mother of God, set up the dichotomy of women as either whores or saints.[84] It is most often a male problem, but there is a form of the complex that plays out similarly for women. In short, the man (or woman) loves and respects his partner so much that he cannot take pleasure from her; he can only give her pleasure. He can only attend her and make certain she is pleased and satisfied in their sexual relationship. He restrains his sexual feelings so that he has difficulty letting himself desire his "Madonna" wife. However, with a woman he does not love and does not respect, he can visualize her as only a sex object for his pleasure and he then can allow himself to get deeply erotic with her and take all the enjoyment he can from her body. He sees her as a "whore" who exists only for his pleasure. The wife is the Madonna, and the other woman is the whore. This could explain why some men can love their wives, but want some other woman for sex. Unfortunately, when many women get married, and especially when they begin having children, they begin to act like the Madonna.

Some women can have sex with their husbands but not reach an orgasm, or they work hard just to have a weak climax. With some stranger whom they hardly know, they are able to "let it all out" and have more incredible sex than they ever have with their husbands. Why is this so? Usually their husbands are controlling males who posture more like a parent with their wives. Their wives experience them as father figures. How can we have good sex with someone who is parental? Could it bring forward from the subconscious the incest taboo? When it comes to sex, we do not want to be a parent, but an erotic animal. If your partner will not let you use erotic language with them, then your partner may be stuck in the parent ego state. Sex that comes from a sense of duty is never as good as sex that comes from intense sexual feelings, which is the definition of lust.[85]

The previously described wife, who did not want her husband to use dirty language with her when they had sex, illustrates the difference between being a mother object and a sex object. If we stop thinking of sexual slang as being dirty and start thinking of these symbols as erotic communication that is translating both our desires and our partner's passion, then this dirty talk actually enriches the sexual relationship and the sexual pleasure. Where did we get the idea that erotic language is dirty? If we look deeper for the answer to that question, we will find that it is dirty simply because it is erotic. Those who promote the negative sexual script feel that propriety should be maintained when having sex. They believe our sexual feelings should be controlled. If you are female, you should not talk like a whore or a slut. You are supposed to be a good girl, not a bad girl. Women should not become like Eve. They should have sex without becoming libidinous. If women get in touch with the bad girl or the whore that is down there with your libido, they are given the message that they might become sexually addicted and ruin their life. That is the message of all the monster moralists who create sexual negativity and erotic fear. How shameful to be sexual! Thank you, Saint Paul, Saint Augustine, and Saint Thomas Aquinas! I certainly do not want to sin with my husband or with my wife. Thank the Church and the conventional culture for keeping me sexually repressed, restricted, and frustrated.

Making Erotica

This brings us around to the title of this chapter, "Making Erotica Instead of Making Love." Love is really more of an emotion than it is a physical act. It is an emotion that contains deep levels of empathy, sensitivity, and affectionate devotion. It is most important that a couple learns how to make emotional love to each other, and it is addressed in chapters 7 and 8, but when it comes to meaningful and pleasurable orgasmic sex, love is not enough. In fact, love is not what is primary to successful peak pleasure in a sexual relationship. What is most important is getting into a deep erotic state, both psychologically and physiologically. That is why "fucking" may be a more helpful symbol than "making love." The first phase of good sex requires focusing on saying and doing what will put you and your partner in a deep erotic state; making erotica. Creating sexual tension and passion is what good sex is about.

The well-known sexual research team of Masters and Johnson became famous for their unique work in researching the process of human sexual response and the treatment of sexual dysfunction. What made their work so unique was the method of research they used. No other sex researchers had ever used direct observation of couples actually having sexual intercourse.

Masters and Johnson observed over ten thousand cycles of intercourse. They discovered very accurate and factual information on physiological responses in couples having sexual intercourse culminating in orgasm.[86] They also studied couples with sexual dysfunction and developed a new approach to sex therapy previously unknown. Their approach to treatment had an 80 percent success rate. From the data of their work, they developed what they entitled the four-phase sexual response cycle, the first of which is the excitement phase[87]. This is one of the most important stages of the cycle. In this first stage, a lot has to happen before a couple starts intercourse. Intercourse should not start until a couple has completed the process of the first stage. The first stage requires both psychological and physiological changes in the couple. The purpose of this excitement stage is to build sexual excitement or sexual tension. Sexual intercourse starts at the second stage, or plateau stage. The third stage is the orgasmic stage. The fourth stage is the resolution stage.

Murray Davis coined terminology to describe the shift that needs to be made from the resolution state when we do not feel sexual desire to the excitement state when we do. She uses the phrase "everyday reality" in contrast to "erotic reality."[88] When we are in a state of everyday reality, we do not feel very sexual or erotic. In daily reality, we are thinking about or doing responsible life maintenance, such as working, cleaning, fixing, shopping, studying, taking care of children, or meeting social and family obligations. None of this sounds very sexy, does it?

In erotic reality, our mind should be focused on sexual pleasure. Our effort is to increase sexual tension and to enjoy erotic pleasure. Our mind is concentrating on the sexual sensations being stimulated. This is the stage where a couple gets into what is popularly called foreplay. We are literally making or creating erotica. We are doing things that stimulate the erogenous zones on each other's anatomy. We are going deep into our libido and surrendering to lust. Psychologically we are giving into our desire to mate. Whatever one says, it should be erotic language. Whatever one does, it should increase sexual tension in oneself and in one's partner.

Getting Sexually Excited

Imagine the excitement stage as being on a scale numbered from one to ten, with ten being close to reaching orgasm. In addition, there are certainly plenty of exceptions to this, but often when the male comes to the female, he is already at six or seven on the scale. The female is often somewhere between one and three. As the couple begins to make the shift from daily reality to erotic reality, the male goes quickly to nine. He wants to enter and start stroking, but his female partner is now only at six. If she prematurely opens the gate before she has built near maximum sexual tension, it is not likely that she will have an orgasm. Her male partner will come and release before she is able to climax. Her male partner will be returning to everyday reality. She will be left unfulfilled and unsatisfied.

What is most important in the excitement phase of the four-phase sexual response cycle is stimulating the physical changes that must take place within our bodies. These changes prepare us so that we can perform adequately and experience maximum pleasure and enjoyment. For the purpose of illustration, let us describe what happens in a female when she starts to kiss and make out with her lover. As she is being kissed and caressed by him, her eyes will begin to dilate, her ear lobes will begin to fill with blood as well as her lips, and they will swell up. At the same time, all the little saliva pores in her mouth will open up and her mouth will become wet with saliva. The nipples on her breasts will become erect and a pink flush will show on her chest. As she is getting deeper into erotic feeling, blood will move into her vaginal area. Whenever there is engorgement of blood, there is heat and her vagina will reach a temperature between 104 and 107 degrees. At the same time, her lips majora and lips minora will swell with blood and take on a rich pink color. The lining of her vaginal walls will also swell with blood and a clear slippery fluid will begin to appear as she becomes more aroused. The sphincter muscle of the outer third of her vagina will become relaxed for easy penetration.

If suddenly her parents came in the front door, her husband came home, a cop shined a flashlight through the window of the car, or her child started to cry, her adrenal glands would secrete adrenalin into her blood stream. She would open her eyes and the blood would move out of her ear lobes and lips. All the pores in her mouth would close and her mouth would become dry. The pink flush on her chest would disappear and the nipples on her breasts would become flax. The engorgement of blood in her pelvic area would move out, closing the pores in her vaginal area. She would dry out and the lips minora and majora would shrink, as the sphincter muscle in her outer third of her vagina would contract shut, making penetration extremely difficult.

A male also has physiological changes similar to the female, but instead of vaginal lubrication, the male has an erection. The point is that, for both men and women, it takes more than just an agreement in order to have satisfying sex. They need the increase of sexual arousal in order to make the physical changes necessary to prepare them for sexual intercourse and orgasm. To have pleasurable feelings and orgasm, each person needs to build sexual tension almost to the point of coming in the excitement phase of the cycle.

Besides physical stimulation and arousal, there is also a need for psychological preparation. Kaplan's sexual response model is different from Masters and Johnsons. She has a three-stage model that starts with desire, then excitement, and then orgasm.[89] How can we have enjoyment and pleasure in sex if we do not have any desire for it? We could explain the lack of desire as "being stuck in daily reality and not being able to make the transition into erotic reality." There are things that couples can do to create desire and to get into a sexual mood.

Learning how to get into a deep erotic state can make for a strong deep bond and a meaningful sexual experience. Great sex does enrich a marriage as it does any relationship.

Shifting From Daily Reality to Erotic Reality

John and Mary have been married for seven years. They have two children. They have a boy who is five years old and a girl who is three years old. They both have MBA degrees and work for large companies across town from each other. They have managerial positions. Mary drives a new Volvo, and John drives a new BMW. Their routine is as follows: Mary gets up in the morning at 6:00 a.m., puts the coffee on, and showers to get ready for work. John, who is a "new age sensitive male," gets up and wakes the kids for breakfast. After he has fed them breakfast, Mary dresses them. The son goes to pre-school and the daughter goes to a nursery. John takes his son to pre-school on the way to work, and Mary takes their daughter to the nursery on her way to work.

Let us just follow Mary's day. She gets to work around 8:15 a.m. She already has messages waiting, which her secretary hands to her. She remembers that she has an important meeting at 8:30 a.m. in which she has to present her marketing goals and objectives in front of her boss and her colleagues. Bill is one of her colleagues who competed with her last year for the advancement that she ended up getting. He is still very angry and feels he should have been offered the position she now has. He is determined to make her look bad in front of her boss. Mary starts to present her project, and Bill starts picking it apart. They adjourned for lunch, and it is 11:30 a.m. Mary's secretary hands her some more messages, calls she needs to return. She picks out the most important calls and returns them. She notices it is now 12:00 p.m., and she has an important lunch meeting with a potential high-end client. She calls him and lets him know that she is on her way. She gets to the meeting late, but they relate well together and the the meeting was successful. They set up another time to meet, and Mary heads back to her office.

In the afternoon meeting, Bill just picks her apart again. He has questions she can't answer without more research, so at the end of the conference everyone agrees to meet again in the morning. Mary assures everyone she'll research and have the answers to some of Bill's questions. It is now a little after 5:00 p.m. She goes to the nursery and picks up her daughter and heads home.

When Mary gets home, John is already there. Mary asks John if he would play with the kids while she makes dinner. At the dinner table, John and Mary cannot talk because the kids do all the talking. The kids also start fighting, one accusing the other of making a face and the other denying it and throwing some food. There is some crying and yelling, but they all get through dinner, though all the interaction has been with the kids and not between John and Mary. Mary tells John that she needs to do some research on the computer and asks John if he would read to the children and give them their baths. He agrees, and Mary goes into the home office to get ready for the morning meeting.

When it becomes time to bathe the kids, there is a hysterical protest. The children want mommy to bathe them, not daddy, and they both begin to have meltdowns, screaming for mommy. Mary comes out and says she will put them down. She bathes them, reads to them, lets them get up to get a drink, tells them a repetitive story, and finally they are down for the night. She goes into her home office again to get ready for the morning meeting.

John has been watching TV and drinking a beer. At a little after ten in the evening, he goes to Mary and asks her how much longer will it be before she can come to bed. She says about twenty minutes more. John gets into bed and reads while waiting for Mary. After a half an hour, Mary comes into the bedroom. John notices how tired and stressed she looks. He asks, "What's wrong with you? You look so stressed." Mary tells him about the meeting and about Bill's hostility with her. John says, "You don't have to take any shit from him; go tell him to fuck himself." Mary gets angry, and says, "That doesn't help at all." John replies again in a parental sounding voice: "Well if you can't take the heat, get out of the kitchen." Mary replies, "What do you mean? Quit my job? And how do we make our house payments and the car payments on your salary? John, you are such an asshole!" John replies, "And you are such a bitch!" Mary climbs into bed and clicks out the light. They lie there in the dark quietly, both with their backs turned toward the other. John rolls over so that he can face Mary's back and asks, "Do you want to make love?" Mary responds, "No, I am too tired." John responds, "You are always too tired. You never want to have sex." Mary replies, "That's not true. We had sex Friday night and Saturday night, and you're the one who said you were too tired on Sunday." John replies, "You never want to do it, and you really keep me sexually frustrated." Mary replies, "You are such an asshole." The conversation ends and they lay there in the dark quietly.

Let us look at a different ending to this story: Mary comes into the bedroom looking tired and stressed. John asks her, "What are you feeling, Mary? You really look tired and stressed." She replies, "It's that Bill. In the meeting today he just kept picking me apart." John replies, "That must really be difficult having to deal with his hostilities toward you in front of the boss and your colleagues." Mary replies, "It was starting to get to me, but I think I am ready for him for tomorrow." John replies, "Let me help you. When you get up in the morning, just get out of here, and I will get the kids up and get them off to school. Let me do that for you. You do so much for us. I think you are just amazing. I am so lucky to have you as my partner and the mother of our children." Then John gets up, takes some body lotion from the dresser and starts to massage Mary's feet. At first she tries to tell him he does not have to do that, but he continues and she gives in. He then does her legs and her back, her neck, and then her arms and her hands. He puts no sexual moves on her. It is a straight honest message. Mary starts to reply, "Oh, that feels so good. You are such a dear. How did I ever find you? You are such a love!" The massage is done. The light goes out. They lay in bed in the quiet dark. Mary turns toward John, puts her hand on his penis, and starts to stroke it. She says, "John, let's make love." They do for almost an hour, and then they fall asleep.

In the first ending to this story, John did not help Mary get out of everyday reality. In the second ending to the story, he obviously did. Sometimes just being empathic and kind toward your partner will turn them on to begin the excitement phase. Sometimes just taking time to listen or play cards or some lighthearted board game together will help make the shift. Spending time talking about sexual feelings or sharing sexual fantasies will start the turn on. Watching a portion of an erotic movie or reading an explicit sexual passage from a novel can trump daily reality and move you into erotic reality. Exercising together and then relaxing with a long conversation that gets you emotionally connected will do the trick. Talk about all the things that are right about your relationship, those things that you find attractive about your partner, or sometimes just come right out and say, "I really want to have sex with you tonight."

Chapter Four:

Female Orgasm: Surrendering to Lust

Besides having to deal with gender discrimination, women have to struggle with a long history of negative conditioning about their sexuality. The negative messages they get from the culture in early childhood makes one wonder why a female would want anything to do with sex. Social conditioning and learning experiences play a major determining role in a woman's sexual response. There is almost universal agreement that a woman's sexual response pattern, as well as her ability to achieve or not achieve orgasm, is primarily based on psychological rather than physiological causes. There are some exceptions to this if the woman is dealing with menopause or hormone issues, but generally a women's difficulty reaching orgasm is both psychologically and educationally based.[90]

What is true for almost everyone in this culture, male and female, is that there is little access to comprehensive sex education. Because of negative sexual scripting, there is almost a complete failure of parents, schools, or anyone to provide books and conversation with accurate information and rational discussion of sexuality. Parents do not feel comfortable with the subject. They are not certain how much information should be told to their children at any age. Even age-appropriate books giving information on sexuality are still removed from school libraries. Information is kept hidden, if allowed at all. At least boys can talk to other boys about sex and even find some porn magazines to get some information, but girls feel they should never be naughty. Since sex is taught as something naughty and dirty, it is often the case that they are not told about it. Many girls also feel that to show an interest in sex is like being a bad person. Often what they are taught is that someday when they grow up, they will get married, and then they can have sex in order to have children. Until then, girls are kept in ignorance, and they are too often admonished for showing an interest in the subject at all. For example, most girls are not told about the clitoris. Masturbation is often viewed as something only a slut or a whore would do. A girl is often not told about it. It is feared by some parents that if a girl learns about her clitoris and starts to masturbate, she will become sexually active, get pregnant, have a terrible reputation, and ruin her life.

Sweden begins sex education at a pre-school level. Sex education is provided through all twelve grades. Contraception is provided for free by the government.[91] The Netherlands also provides free contraception to teens. Neither the Netherlands nor Sweden teach abstinence, and both these countries have the lowest teen pregnancy rate among industrialized nations.[92] In America, boys are striving to get laid and lose their virginity. Girls are taught to preserve their virginity until marriage. Although boys are taught not to have sex until marriage, they are not made to feel that maleness means to wait until marriage. Boys do not have to worry about their reputations. When they get to high school, they may get a reputation as a playboy or a stud. However, a girl can hardly survive socially if she is tagged as a slut or a whore.[93] Good girls are virgins until marriage. Think about the negative scripting to control their sexuality. This "virgin doctrine" for Western Civilization is rooted in the Virgin Mary, who is still highly promoted as the ideal for all women. The Eve propaganda can also contribute to a girl's inhibition and fear of her sexuality. Even the celibacy vows for priests and nuns suggest that to abstain from all sexual pleasure is somehow a virtue, even though it is obviously abnormal and unnatural. Boys discover the pleasure of their penis very early and start to masturbate and experience orgasm as soon as they are able. Most girls never masturbate. They do not even know about such a thing. They usually learn about it from a boyfriend. It is not surprising to learn how many women do not have sex because they feel it is dirty and wrong. It is even more surprising how many women are not able to experience orgasm, or they have but not with any consistency.[94]

Women were told so many confusing messages about their sexuality, from the New Testament belief that they were transgressors because they had Eve's disposition to the medieval fear of women as witches and psychics. During the Victorian period, they were not to have any sexual feelings at all! Their bodies had to be hidden from men, so that they would not cause a man to sin as Eve caused Adam to sin.

The Female Orgasmic Controversy

Historically, there has been a controversy over female orgasm. Women who could not have an orgasm were called frigid. A frigid woman was thought of as a block of ice. No one dared to get close to her. There were passionate women labeled frigid because they could not reach orgasm. The passionately frigid woman was a woman who liked men and loved sex. They could get "hot and wet" and respond warmly and affectionately, but always stopped short of having a climax. Are you going to call her frigid? We have finally learned so much about female orgasm that we no longer use that icy cold word for women who cannot come or cannot come with any regularity. The term I prefer is pre-orgasmic. Pre-orgasmic means that a woman has not had an orgasm yet, but she can if she is willing to learn how. Research has now found the information that enables women to become orgasmic if they want to experience sexual fulfillment.

Let us go back in history to the female orgasmic controversy. It was started by Sigmund Freud, MD. He taught that women had two kinds of orgasms. They had clitoral orgasms and they could have vaginal orgasms. He made a value judgment saying that the clitoral orgasm was an immature orgasm because it did not require a penis for stimulating it. The vaginal orgasm was more mature because it was stimulated by the male phallus.[95] He then went further in his judgments. He taught that women who could not reach orgasm or could only experience an orgasm through stimulation of the clitoris had deep-seated unconscious anger and hostility toward their fathers. When having sex, they could not surrender to the male penis because it represented their father's maleness. Freud believed that only a vaginal orgasm was mature and acceptable. Think about what this meant. It was not good enough for a woman to have an orgasm unless it was a vaginal orgasm stimulated by the male penis. Women who achieved orgasm from stimulation of their clitoris were immature and had not resolved subconscious issues with their fathers. Clitoral orgasms were not acceptable and women were made to feel guilty about having the wrong kind of orgasm. The cure for this problem of being frigid was to get into psychoanalysis and work out one's issues with her father. The belief was that if she did that, she could then have vaginal orgasms and be sexually fulfilled.

Another player in the female orgasmic controversy was a woman psychoanalyst by the name of Marie Robinson, MD. She took Freud's theory about the two orgasms and wrote an excellent book called *The*

Power of Sexual Surrender.[96] What made her book so valuable was her ability to take the technical academic style of Freud and communicate his theory with wonderful illustrations so that anyone with a high school education could read and understand what Freud was saying. She used examples from her case files of women who grew up with fathers they didn't get along with and ended up in adult life unable to have an orgasm or only being able to have a clitoral orgasm. Like Dr. Freud, she believed that the vaginal orgasm was the only legitimate orgasm for women. Again, the cure for not being orgasmic or only being able to come with her clitoris was to get into psychoanalysis, which could take about five years of treatment to correct. Dr. Robinson's book became very popular. It made the best-selling list in non-fiction, and many women got into treatment to resolve sexual dysfunction. For Robinson, the woman must resolve her subconscious resistance to surrendering to the male in order to achieve a vaginal orgasm.[97]

The Important Use of the Pubococcygeus Muscle

Arnold Kegel, MD, a gynecologist from the University of Southern California School of Medicine and a professor emeritus, was researching and treating women who were suffering from urinary incontinence. Urinary incontinence is a problem that can cause much social embarrassment. Whenever a woman with this problem laughs, coughs, sneezes, or makes any sudden movement, she involuntarily voids urine. There was no real cure for this problem.

In female anatomy, there is a band of muscle that connects to the tailbone or coccyx, stretches between the legs, and connects to the pubic bone. This band of muscle is therefore called the pubococcygeus muscle. There are three canal openings in this band of muscle, and a sphincter controls each canal opening: the urinary sphincter, the vaginal sphincter, and the anal sphincter. Kegel discovered that if the pubococcygeus muscle is weak, it could not squeeze the urinary sphincter tight enough to keep from voiding urine whenever it is pressured. The problem was trying to figure out how to strengthen the pubococcygeus muscle. No known exercise could strengthen this muscle. Women who were physically fit and in good condition could have a weak pubococcygeus muscle. Women who were in poor condition and even obese could have a strong muscle. Kegel developed exercises that would strengthen the muscle. They have become known as the Kegel squeezes. After having his patients who suffered from urinary incontinence do the Kegel exercises or squeezes, he achieved very significant results. Many of the women stopped involuntarily voiding urine. In addition, something surprisingly new developed. Many of the women mentioned to Kegel that they had an orgasm for the first time. Others told stories that they were achieving more orgasms than usual.

At first Kegel thought the association of achieving orgasm with the urinary incontinent exercises was just a coincidence, but the comments from women attesting to a relationship between the exercises and sexual climax finally convinced him to investigate female orgasm. Kegel took a group of one thousand women who were diagnosed by clinicians as non-orgasmic, and who by their own testimony had never experienced an orgasm. He then taught them the exercises or squeezes. In addition, he explained to them the importance of building an orgasmic platform. The orgasmic platform is similar to the excitement stage in Masters and Johnson's four-phase sexual response cycle discussed in chapter three. In order to reach orgasm, a woman needs to get in a deep erotic state to create the physiological changes necessary to reach orgasm. The orgasmic platform has to do with making those changes. In particular, the swelling of the inner lining of her vaginal walls that is created by blood flow when she gets into a deep erotic state. Kegel taught these women in his research group to focus on erotic sensations to deepen and intensify their sexual feelings. He educated them about the physiological changes that have to take place to reach orgasm. He taught them the importance of getting in heat so that the blood would flow to the pelvic area. This blood flow enables the lips majora and minora to swell with blood and start lubrication to flow from the pores. This process also causes the walls of the vaginal canal to fill with blood and become moist and warm. The vaginal sphincter will relax and the clitoris will erect and fill with blood. He also taught the women to focus on increasing sexual tension. Six hundred and fifty of the one thousand women achieved their first orgasm. Sixty-five percent is significant research.[98]

What makes the Kegel squeezes or exercises so important is that in the vaginal canal there are no nerve endings related to sexual stimulation. The only area for sexual stimulation in the vagina is in the outer third of the organ. A woman can feel sexual sensation behind the vaginal sphincter. If you put firm pressure behind the ring of the muscle or sphincter, a woman will feel pleasurable sensation. If you visualize the vaginal muscle as a clock, the area of sensation would be between four and eight o'clock on the dial. Some women report sensation all around the dial.[99] Kegel believed the pubococcygeus needed to be in good condition so that a woman can squeeze on the penis and feel more sensation in intercourse. He felt that women were not feeling all the sensation they could feel if their muscle was not strong or if they were not using it in intercourse.[100]

What is most important about Kegel's research is that these women were not treated with psychotherapy. They were just given comprehensive sex education that included information about their body and how it functions sexually. Kegel felt that what most women need to become orgasmic is education, not therapy.[101] His research questioned the need for psychotherapy for pre-orgasmic women and supported a view that what most women needed was education to teach them how to have sex.[102] For most women, the issue is not about their relationship with their fathers, but rather the ignorance that our culture teaches about being sexual. This is the negative sexual scripting to keep women from enjoying too much sex!

Masters and Johnson's research ended the orgasmic controversy. Their research produced hard data on the physiology of intercourse, which was revolutionary for their time. What they found that ended the orgasmic controversy was the fact that women do not have two kinds of orgasms. They only have one kind of orgasm, but they have many erogenous zones that can trigger their orgasm. Masters and Johnson recorded some ten thousand female orgasms and found that when a woman has an orgasm there are always pelvic contractions.[103] Some women can reach orgasm just through stimulation of their breasts or the nipples of their breasts. Some can come from deep kissing. Some can come from clitoral stimulation, and some can come through intercourse. There are women who have orgasms in their sleep triggered by an erotic dream.

Whatever the trigger, the orgasm is always the same physiological response: pelvic contractions. With each contraction, there is a surge of pleasurable feeling and a release of sexual tension. There is one orgasm and many different triggers. Masters and Johnson also found that the most intense orgasms came through masturbation, not sexual intercourse. The primary "hot button" or erogenous zone for all women is the clitoris. The majority of women, up to 80 percent, reach orgasm through clitoral stimulation. Even in intercourse, the movement of the fatty tissue around the clitoris caused by the stroking can stimulate the clitoris to orgasm.

Masters and Johnson taught that women should not surrender to their male partner. They were adamant that a woman should surrender to her own lust.[104] She should focus on erotic sensation and surrender to those feelings. When the neurons related to sexual orgasm are stimulated to reach their threshold, they will automatically explode into orgasm. A woman does not reach orgasm by thinking about having one. She will reach orgasm when she builds enough sexual tension to fire the orgasmic neurons. In order to build sexual tension, she does not focus on her partner, but rather on her own erogenous zones that stimulate sexual tension. Whatever a woman does when having sex, it should be increasing sexual pleasure and tension. It is equally important that whatever her partner is doing does not distract her from building erotic excitement. If he is disturbing her sensate focus, she should tell him. When having sex, there should be nothing going on that is distracting or breaking one's focus on building sexual tension. Anything that is spoken should be spoken in erotic language to maintain sexual feeling.

In the discussion on masturbation in chapter five, it will be pointed out how masturbation is helpful as an excellent training method for learning how to be erotically focused. Being able to masturbate to orgasm teaches you how to focus on and surrender to lust. When having sexual intercourse, you transfer into your relationship what you do when you have sex with yourself. When you are masturbating, you are really doing a form of self-foreplay. When having sex with a partner, a woman needs just as much or more foreplay to get into erotic reality at a level that prepares her for orgasm when intercourse begins. Foreplay is one of the most important activities couples need to prolong when having sex with each other.

The G-Spot

Lastly, we need to recognize Whipple and Perry as the two people who brought to popular attention the controversial "G-spot." They did not discover the G-spot; they were the researchers who brought it to everyone's attention. In the 1950s, a gynecologist by the name of Grafenberg discovered the G-spot. After he died, Whipple and Perry named the spot after him and published a book on the G-spot that created quite a controversy.[105] Today there is still some debate about just what it is and whether it is real. The consensus is that some women have a G-spot. Some people belief that all women have a G-spot, but they have not discovered it yet; it is simply asleep.

So, what is the G-spot? It is another erogenous zone that some women have discovered along the anterior wall of the vagina. It is located about an inch or so into the front wall of the outer third of the vagina. For some women, stimulation of this area can trigger orgasm. Often accompanying the orgasm is an ejaculation of a clear fluid.[106] This fluid neither looks nor smells like urine. It does not stain sheets like urine. This fluid has been tested in a laboratory and found not to be urine. One can buy a G-spot finder through a sex accessory store. It is a little tool that will help you reach and stimulate the G-spot area. The tool may help awaken one's G-spot.

Masters and Johnson felt a woman who could reach orgasm in masturbation but not in intercourse was sexually dysfunctional. If she could reach orgasm in intercourse but not in masturbation, she was sexually dysfunctional. If she could not reach orgasm at all, she was considered sexually dysfunctional. In other words, a fully sexually functioning woman who is liberated from the negative sexual scripting by the culture enjoys having sex with herself, as well as with a partner. She can reach orgasm with her self and with her partner.[107]

Getting into Erotica to Become Erotic

For a woman to be able to fulfill herself sexually, she must learn to enjoy the pleasure centers her body has for her. She must free herself from inhibition, fear, and embarrassment. In order to accomplish this, she needs to be reading and viewing erotic material: books, magazines, and films. Sex should be on her mind. She must come to a place where she gives herself permission to have sexual pleasure with herself, as well as with someone else. She has to learn how to surrender to her lust, desire, and sexual sensations she experiences when having sex. A woman should not focus as much on her partner, but rather on the erotic sensations she is feeling. She surrenders to her libido. She includes in her self-definition the awareness that she is an erotic, sexual person who is competent and capable of giving and receiving sexual pleasure. She must give herself permission to have sexual thoughts and fantasies. Erotic film and erotic reading material can be profoundly helpful in this area.

A woman also needs to learn to get comfortable with the use of erotic language. It is much more difficult to have an orgasm when your mind is heavily guarded against anything sexual. For that matter, it is difficult to even desire to have sex when you keep your heart "clean" and your mind "pure." Good girls have a harder time enjoying sex than bad girls. A major struggle for women today is also the overwhelming sense of responsibility for family and career. The difficulty balancing these responsibilities with relaxation and time for oneself prevents a focus on erotic pleasure.

Women have been more influenced by the Adam and Eve mythology of the Book of Genesis than they realize. The Eve scripting has been in Western Culture since the first century. Remember, Saint Paul talked about Eve being the "transgressor." Saint Augustine and Saint Thomas Aquinas expanded on that idea in their teachings. This fear of being like Eve is what helps fuel the double standard between men and women in our culture. A male who enjoys his sexuality is not seen as a slut or a whore. A woman who enjoys her sexuality risks having those derogatory labels attached to her reputation.[108]

Think how different it would be for women if a different interpretation of Eve were to be presented. Eve, in my opinion, was adventurous and intelligent. She found the Garden of Eden really boring. It was beautiful but not exciting. In fact, she had learned that being good all the time was also boring. She needed more. Eve was a woman with ambition! She was a woman who had insight and awareness of her sexuality. She thought that if the Lord designed the clitoris, He must have meant for her to use it. Surely if the Lord created sexuality, He created it for a purpose. Eve took a risk that gave to her life and Adam's adventure and excitement. Most of all, she gave Adam more pleasure than he had ever received in that damn garden! Although they were forced out of the Garden of Eden, they gained the pleasure of their sexuality, and in addition, they had great enjoyment having children. After they left the garden, they never looked back. In fact, they never missed the Garden of Eden. They had each other and their children. Had it not been for Eve taking a risk, they would just have had the monotony of the garden. Without eve doing what she did, not only would we not have our sexuality, none of us would have been born.

Eve should be every woman's heroine. She was the first feminist. She sexually liberated herself and Adam. She was condemned for all time, but think of who condemned her: the negative sexual script moralists. The lesson from Eve, then, is that if women want to be sexually liberated, they need to get out of the garden of conventional thinking and break their commitment to propriety. It will take some work and experience to ever become sexually self-actualized. For women especially, allowing themselves to be deviant from the teachings of the negative script conditioning is difficult.

Chapter Five:

Masturbation:
Becoming Erotic with Yourself

You may recall from chapter one that the Egyptians celebrated masturbation in honor of their creator god Atum. They believed that the creation of the universe began from his ejaculate. Masturbation was not a negative issue for the Egyptians. On the other hand, the official position on masturbation in the Catholic Church is that masturbation is a mortal sin. Venial sins are pardonable in the Church; they are like misdemeanors. Mortal sins are like felonies that bring on a sentence of death. In 1976, the Vatican declared that masturbation is an "intrinsically and seriously disordered act." Again in 1993, Pope John Paul II condemned masturbation as morally wrong. Likewise, in the Protestant churches, most fundamentalist Christians condemn masturbation as sinful and morally wrong.[109] In matters of sexuality, Christian churches traditionally have had great difficulty. While they make a significant contribution to charity and others' welfare, there appears to be an obsession with sexual issues more than any other subject. That makes it difficult not to be critical of the negative script they keep reinforcing.

There are also people who are not Christian who feel negatively about masturbation. Where did their negative feelings come from? They certainly did not come from the Egyptians! The negativity about masturbation is another symptom created by the advocates of the negative sexual script to control sexual activity and sexual pleasure. Do you remember in 1994 when President Clinton fired Surgeon General Jocelyn Elders when she said on television that masturbation should be taught as part of human sexuality?[110] What was so bad about that? Who did it offend, and why?

Who are the people behind the outrage to silence her? They are all the authorities and institutions from the Middle Ages to this twenty-first century that have helped to further fear, guilt, shame, inhibition, and ignorance about anything sexual. They are the writers and advocates of the negative sexual script.

Onan and Genesis 38:7–10

There is no teaching in the Bible about masturbation. Jesus makes no mention of it. There is one Old Testament passage that is continually corrupted by clergymen, priests, and laymen. The passage is found in the Book of Genesis. chapter 38:7–10. In the story, the Lord kills Er, the first-born son of Judah. Judah directs Onan, his second son, to "go in unto thy brother's wife and perform the duty of a husband, and raise up seed to thy brother." However, Onan does not want to father children who would be raised as Ers. "Thus it came to pass, when he went into his brother's wife, that he spilled his seed on the ground, lest he should give seed to his brother. And the thing which he did was evil in the sight of the Lord and the Lord slew him also."

Some people have taken this passage to mean that masturbation is wrong. Others have interpreted this passage as condemning coitus interruptus, the withdrawal method of birth control. That is really what Onan actually did. Jewish scholars interpret the condemnation of Onan in this passage as Onan's disobedience and deception in not following the Jewish tradition of fathering his brother's children.[111]

It is important to remember that the Old Testament is a Jewish book, not a Christian book. It was written by Jews for Jews several centuries before Christianity came into existence. Therefore, I think we should accept Jewish scholarship on this matter. To interpret this passage as God's condemnation of masturbation, or the use of birth control, is again taking a verse out of its context and true meaning and exploiting it for one's own bias view.

The Reverend Balthazar Becker coined the term "Onanism" as a synonym for the word masturbation. He wrote a pamphlet in 1710 entitled, "Onania, the Heinous Sin of Self-Pollution and All Its Frightful Consequences for Both Sexes, Considered with Spiritual and Physical Advice."[112] Other pamphlets followed written by noted physicians who were the best authorities of their time.

Samuel David Tissot, MD, was a European medical doctor and a devout Catholic who believed that masturbation was not only morally wrong as the Church taught, but that it was also seriously injurious to physical health. He taught that the loss of semen would destroy health. He saw masturbation as self-abuse, since it evolved the habitual loss of semen, which would be harmful to one's health.[113]

When Sex Was Wrongly Believed to Be Unhealthy

Benjamin Rush, the founder of American psychiatry and President George Washington's personal physician, published an article and taught that masturbation caused mental illness, epilepsy, impotence, and even death.[114] Other physicians followed, and it became a false belief that many illnesses, diseases, and unexplained symptoms were the result of Onania, self-abuse or masturbation. Medicine joined religion in condemning masturbation. Medical doctors, priests, and ministers condemned the practice as destructive to one's health and to one's soul. B.G. Jefferis MD, PhD published a book called *Safe Counsel*, which went through thirty-nine editions between 1893 and 1928. The book was very condemning of masturbation as a health hazard.[115]

In his book, Jefferis gave what is now known to be totally false and incorrect information. His book, and other books like his, was read by millions of people. Jefferis and countless others at the time taught that the fluid of the testes contained important nutrition that one's body must have to maintain and protect what we would call today the immune system. The belief was that whenever a male would ejaculate, he would be discharging the "healthy" fluids made by the testes, which were needed to maintain the health of his own body. It was taught that the loss of semen would make him vulnerable for developing disease and physical weakness. He would literally go blind, lose all physical strength, suffer dementia, develop epilepsy, or even tuberculosis.

For women, masturbation would cause brain damage, which in turn could cause blindness or dementia. It could subject them to attacks of hysteria, stomach pain, ulceration of the uterus, or elongation of the clitoris, which Tissot believed would deprive them of modesty and reason.[116]

In America, J.F. Kellogg, MD, played an important role in the anti-masturbation crusade. He went around the country lecturing about the dangers to the health of those who did this evil thing. He developed corn flakes as a food that would help restore the nutrition that was lost from the discharge when masturbating. He also believed that corn flakes were bland enough to curb sexual desire and therefore lessen the desire to masturbate.[117] The current belief during the anti-masturbation crusade was that spicy foods stimulated sexual desire. It was recommended that one should eat bland foods. One should not eat meat, since it was believed that meat would stimulate sexual desire. The Reverend Sylvester Graham, who encouraged the use of whole-wheat flour to replace lost nutrition from masturbation, still has his name on the Graham cracker.[118]

Frightened parents bought appliances designed to keep children from being able to touch their genitals. They bought devices like a wire cage that locked around a child, like jockey shorts, so that a child could not touch himself or herself. There were about twenty or more contraptions invented to prevent masturbation. There were also many treatment methods taught to cure masturbation: everything from cages, to electrical shock, to putting pure carbolic acid on the clitoris, to tying a child's hands. Using pins to close the foreskin or sewing the foreskin shut to prevent erections and using injections of silver nitrate into the urethra for cauterization were all recommended.[119]

This crusade went even beyond masturbation. Married couples were told not to have sex more than a dozen times a year. It was believed that any sexual excess would be harmful. It was also believed that the "violent" contractions from orgasm damaged the brain, the cardiovascular system, and the nervous system. Most of society was deluded by the most respected and trusted social leaders.

Too many of the clergy, teachers, and doctors supported these false ideas. Some authorities did not join the crusade and did not get on the "anti-masturbation bandwagon." Two of the most recognized were Dr. Havelock Ellis MD, and Dr. Sigmund Freud MD.[120] The anti-masturbation leaders of this movement were deluded but convinced. They deluded much of the populace. Their teachings and beliefs were fallacious and erroneous, but Americans in general became fearful and paranoid about self-abuse. Those who dared to masturbate were believed to be mentally ill. It was thought that they were immoral, sick, and disturbed. A social stigma developed making anything sexual embarrassing to mention. It became shameful to talk about sex or even be seen reading about the subject. It was difficult to find any information on sexuality. The subject was censored and hidden. It was feared that having sexual information or even just talking about sex might cause sexual stimulation, which would ultimately be deleterious.

Medical science came to the realization that these beliefs were pathological and false, but society and culture continued to ignore the findings of medical science. When Alfred Kinsey published his survey on male sexuality in 1948, there was an overwhelming negative response.[121] Much of what his survey said was profoundly disturbing to many Americans. One of the surprising findings was how many Americans said that they masturbated. Even more enlightening was the awareness that this high volume of masturbators was not getting sick and dropping dead. Nothing abnormal was happening to them. In fact, they were responsible citizens. They worked and contributed to the good of society. They had none of the symptoms attributed to masturbation. Medical science had found answers for the symptoms that had been wrongly related to Onanism. Once medical science discovered germs and bacteria, they could not find any harm to a person's health from masturbating. Furthermore, science gained the capability to study semen. They found that the ejaculate was just a fluid to help transport sperm. It had no health benefit.

Reasons for Masturbating

We now know that masturbation is not harmful; in fact, it is helpful to our physical and psychological health. We would all be healthier and happier if we practiced masturbation throughout our whole lifespan. I have compiled twenty reasons why masturbation is so helpful to individuals, couples, and society:

1) Masturbation is pleasurable.

It is most important that people of every age have pleasure in their life. When you are having pleasure, you are feeling good about living. You are enjoying life. We all have stress, pain, and suffering in our lives. Pleasure is an important counterbalance to the stress and struggle of living. Humans, adults and children, can endure incredible stress and suffering if it is counterbalanced with pleasure, joy, and meaning. Sexual orgasm is the ultimate pleasure experience. If you can have orgasmic experiences with yourself, you will actually enjoy nonsexual experiences more. It is the ultimate pleasure that gives you permission to experience other nonsexual pleasures. Pleasure is the light that releases you from the darkness in life.

2) Masturbation releases sexual tension.

We are sexual beings. We were designed like all other living things to procreate. Each of us has a biological mating urge or desire to mate. We are biologically hardwired to be sexually aroused and turned on to desiring sex. It is normal and natural to experience lust; this creates sexual tension that can keep us from being able to sleep, concentrate, or focus on something important, or just plain relax. Masturbation gives us an easy way to release sexual tension.

3) Masturbation releases stressful tension.

Masturbation can act as a relaxation technique. Everyday reality can be stressful, causing a buildup of anxieties and worries. Tensions related to things you have to do or things that you feel went wrong with your day can leave you in a stressful state. You can be bothered with relationship issues and family affairs. When you move from these daily realities to erotic reality, something changes. All the daily reality issues disappear into the background, and erotic thoughts and fantasies come into the foreground. Erotic thoughts and feelings trump the stressors of everyday life. It puts you in a different mental and emotional state. Many people find masturbating just before going to sleep helps give the relaxation needed to fall asleep.

4) Masturbation improves sexual capability and competency.

I believe that masturbation is the first step toward sexual competency. Through having sex with yourself, you can learn how to respond to sexual stimuli. It helps you learn how to put yourself into a deep state of erotic arousal. It is one of the most helpful ways to work out inhibitions, guilt, and fears about surrendering totally to your sexual desire. You can learn how to have an orgasm. You can also learn how to reach a climax more frequently and efficiently. Masturbation is a wonderful hands-on (the pun is intended) way to practice shifting from daily reality to erotic reality. It is the best preparation for having sex with a partner. Much of what you do in masturbation can transfer into a relationship with a partner. Imagine a woman who kept her vow to be abstinent until marriage. She has never masturbated and has never had an orgasm. Then imagine a woman who has kept her vow to be abstinent until marriage, but masturbated regularly to orgasm during her single years. Which of these two women would be most competent on her wedding night? Which would be the most relaxed and responsive to her husband's touching? Which one is most likely to experience an orgasm on her wedding night?

5) Masturbation maintains sexual functioning and sexual fitness.

Masturbation keeps one tuned up sexually. It keeps a person mindful of his or her sexuality so that it does not become lost in everyday reality. Masters and Johnson have said that our sexual system needs to be exercised and used regularly if it is to keep functioning and not dry up, especially as we age. As we grow older, our libido starts to diminish. Masters and Johnson used the phrase "use it or lose it" when referring to sexual ability and growing old.[122]

6) Masturbation helps maintain a healthy prostate gland.

Whenever a male ejaculates, he is flushing out all the impurities in the pores of the prostate gland. This makes for a healthier prostate gland.[123]

7) Masturbation provides an alternative form of sexual experience.

There are actually two kinds of sexual experiences, solo sex and social sex. Both are enjoyable, but they are different. One is not better than the other. They are each unique, pleasurable experiences. There are advantages and disadvantages to either experience. For example, with solo sex you do not have to negotiate with a partner. You can fully focus and concentrate on your desire only. In social sex, you have the pleasure of experiencing your partner's responses, which can enhance the reality of the event.

8) Masturbation provides a private and personal meaning with yourself.

We all have a relationship with ourselves. We have personal fantasies, dreams, wishes, fears, feelings, and joys. We all have a sense of life spirit; a life energy that is our inner self. We have a sexual relationship with ourselves. Often our very first erotic experience is imprinted in our psyche. We are able to recall all our erotic experiences and even fantasies of new experiences. Sex with our self is a private meeting with our inner being, a very personal pleasure that is like a mystical experience. It is a very spiritual experience. No other experience in life gives you the sense of connection between your body and your spirit as you have when having an orgasm. The mind and the body are truly one, a mystical, spiritual meaning with yourself. It is both private and personal. Masturbation requires an intercommunication with yourself.

9) Masturbation is practical and convenient.

It is not always practical, convenient, or even possible to have social sex. You may not have a suitable partner. Your partner may be sick. Your partner may be feeling too tired. Your partner may be busy working. Your partner may be on a trip. Your partner may not be in the mood. You may be on a trip and are alone without a partner. Masturbation is so practical and convenient! The only person you have to negotiate with for sex is you with yourself. That should not be very difficult. You can simply have sex when you feel like it. If you are a single person, you can still have a meaningful sex life with yourself.

10) Masturbation provides an alternative form of sexual variety with your partner.

Masturbating with your partner or mutually masturbating each other can be a very intimate sexual experience. There is something shared in that experience that is more personal than what is shared in sexual intercourse. You are allowing your partner to see your most private sex life; the sex life you usually keep out of view and hidden from your partner. In addition, during times when you cannot have intercourse with your partner (i.e., immediately after your partner has given birth to a baby or when treating a vaginal yeast infection) mutual masturbation can provide a very pleasurable sexual experience. In addition, if the male should reach orgasm first, he can masturbate his female partner to satisfaction. In cases where the male cannot get an erection, he can still satisfy his female partner.

11) Masturbation eliminates the fear and risk of pregnancy.

Masturbation can be a source for sexual pleasure and release when a couple has no safe means of birth control.

12) Masturbation saves on the cost of birth control.

Birth control is expensive, especially for teenagers and young people.

13) Masturbation can be helpful in "saving" a person's virginity.

For couples that want to wait until marriage before they have intercourse, mutual masturbation can help them release sexual tension without violating their vow to keep virginity until marriage.

14) Masturbation eliminates the risk of getting a sexually transmitted infection.

If you do not know your partner's sexual history and want to protect yourself from getting a sexually transmitted infection, masturbation could be a way to release sexual tension without the risk of getting an infection.

15) Masturbation has no interpersonal risks.

There are no interpersonal risks in having sex with yourself. There are no hurt feelings of rejection or guilt from failure to please your partner. In masturbation, you have none of the politics of interpersonal relating that can make a sexual experience negative and unrewarding.

16) Masturbation provides a sexual experience with no performance anxiety.

There is no performance pressure in masturbation, as one can feel in social sex. There is no need to fake an orgasm. There is no need to worry whether you look presentable. There is no problem or fear of sexual dysfunction, like getting it up, keeping it up, or being able to release at the appropriate time.

17) Masturbation provides the most intense orgasms.

Masters and Johnson's studies found that in masturbation, we have the strongest orgasms. Because there are no distractions of a partner, we can stay focused directly on what arouses us. We can stimulate ourselves to peak excitement without having to negotiate with a partner.

18) Masturbation helps prevent sex crimes.

When Denmark legalized pornography, there was a 68 percent drop in sex crimes. When Japan did the same, rapes fell from 4,677 per year to 1,500 per year. In America, the states that have the greatest access to pornography have had a 53 percent drop in sex crime. The states with the least access to pornography have had an increase in sex crime by 27 percent. Because masturbation is a sexual-tension outlet, it helps prevent sex crime.[124]

19) Masturbation can help relieve cramps during menstruation.

Orgasm helps reduce pelvic congestion and vasocongestion that cause menstrual cramps. When a woman is having menstrual cramps, masturbating to orgasm will often relieve the cramps.

20) Masturbation is important to maintain good health.

Sex scientists have discovered that sexual orgasms have healing power. Sex can improve the immune system. It releases antioxidants. Sex can relieve pain. Orgasms release endorphins, which are a natural painkiller. Orgasm can stop headaches, relieve tension, and make us feel better psychologically.

Studies done by Beverly Whipple, PhD, an associate professor at Rutgers University, found that "orgasm is a natural analgesic." Her research with women suffering from chronic arthritis and other painful conditions found that masturbating to orgasm or achieving orgasm through intercourse and just getting in a deep erotic state improved their threshold for pain.[125] We have come to the realization that masturbation is not just harmless; it is actually helpful to our health.[126] It is especially helpful to our sexual health. Masturbation should be taught as a part of our sexuality. It should also be taught as something that is very important to our physical health and our psychological well-being.

Masturbation should be our first sexual experience. We should start our sexual journey with solo sex. After we have learned how to put ourselves into a deep erotic state and have orgasms, we are then ready for social sex. While we may not be emotionally and psychologically ready for sex with someone else, we can be rehearsing and preparing for sex with a partner by having sex with ourselves. When we meet the right partner and feel ready for sex, we can transfer much of what we have learned in masturbation into our relational experience. That is another reason why masturbation should be taught as something helpful.

Chapter Six:

Male Sexuality:
Pornography, Performance, and Pleasure

David and Lisa have been married for five years. Lisa does not like pornography and has never masturbated. She cannot feel like having sex unless she feels closely connected to David. She only likes the traditional sexual position of the man on top. Rear entry is out of the question. Her belief is that the "doggie" position is for dogs, not humans. She does not like oral sex. She believes the penis was designed to be put in a vagina and no place else. She does not like it when David tries to stimulate her orally. She thinks she has experienced orgasm but is not certain.

David has had five years of sexual frustration. He feels sexual tension every day. Most of the time his sexual advances toward Lisa are rejected by her. Although he believes it is wrong, he finds himself masturbating several times a week. The truth is he has more sex with himself than he does with his wife. He senses Lisa's discomfort and inhibitions. He has had to inhibit his responses and hold back experimenting with things he feels are sexually exciting. He hides his practice of looking at pornography because he knows that Lisa would never approve.

Although he is sexually frustrated, he still loves Lisa and wants to have children with her and start a family. Paradoxically he continually thinks of having sex with other women. In his sexual fantasies, the fantasy woman desires sex as much as he does, or even more than he does. It is as if David has two lives; one life is the real life he has with Lisa, which is stable and grounded in family values. Lisa is instrumental in helping him create a home. Her income from her work combined with his enable them to have dinners out, a comfortable life, a nice house, a yard, and a car. Together they have made a nest. They enjoy friends. They enjoy each other's families. They plan holidays together. They give each other mutual support and help with all the maintenance that living requires. They help each other with the doubts, fears, and issues that come up from time to time. If you asked David if he loved Lisa, it would be a definite yes.

David's other life is mostly fantasy. He has erotic tension everyday. There is hardly a day he does not desire to have sex with a woman. He would like it to be with Lisa, but most of the time Lisa does not seem to be feeling sexual. David sees real, live women every day on the street and at his office. For him, sex is everywhere. He has some male friends and some colleagues at work who are often telling sexual jokes or stories about getting laid. Often they talk about who they would like to fuck if they could. This other world of David's is an erotic world. It is mostly fantasy, but it is still real because he feels sexual frustration everyday. He usually gets release from this sexual tension by masturbating in private. David finds pornography helpful in bringing him to a stronger orgasm. Although he wants to have sex with Lisa, the chronic rejections at his advances have made him turn more to having sex with himself. David finds that pornography is a helpful fantasy partner. Enriching his sexual relationship with himself enables him to better accept the sexual frustration he feels with Lisa. He finds himself less angry and resentful. He compensates for their sexual differences with porn and masturbation. This seems to keep him from sexually acting out and having an affair.

Lisa often goes to bed before David. She gets tired and David stays up to watch the late show on television. Often though, when Lisa goes to bed, David will watch pornography on his computer and have sex with himself. He then feels relaxed and can fall asleep almost immediately. One night while David is watching porn on his computer, Lisa gets up to get a drink of water and catches him looking at pornography. She is shocked, to say the least. she feels angry, hurt, and offended. She feels complete disapproval. She feels a rush of confusion and sorrow. She has always thought so highly of David. She had no idea he could do something like watch pornography. For Lisa, it is as if she had caught David with another woman. Her reaction is as if she had just found out he had been having affairs behind her back. She asks him how long he has been watching porn and if he has ever had a real affair. With tears and resentment, she tells David how she could never compete with one of those women in the porn video and asks how he can look at women as sexual objects. David feels so much shame, embarrassment, and guilt that he confesses that he watches porn and masturbates four or five times a week and occasionally more. Lisa feels he is sexually addicted and insists that he go for sexual addiction treatment. Finally, after a long discussion, they agree to go first to a marriage counselor.

The story of David and Lisa is not unique. Many of the clients who come into marriage counseling tell a similar story. The husband or boyfriend is found out that he is into pornography. The wife or girlfriend is usually very upset and threatened by the discovery that her man needs to look at sex. What often makes the female more perplexed is the recognition that although she feels they have a great sex life together, he still looks at other women and enjoys or needs to look at pictures or videos of women having sex. Most women have a very difficult time understanding why pornography is so important to men.

The Complexity of Male Sexuality

Male sexuality is very complex. Not only do most women not understand it, most men do not either. In the twenty- five years that I have been teaching human sexuality, I have greatly increased my own understanding. Teaching the subject helped me better understand my own sexuality. Regarding heterosexual male sexuality, there is one axiom that I have found to be almost universally agreed upon by most men. In discussions with heterosexual men, it seems that it is an accepted general truth that most men feel great sexual frustration. In fact, most men feel sexual frustration almost everyday. Males have what appears to be a hypersensitivity to sexuality. Males were biologically hard-wired to plant their seed everywhere they can. Nature, or if you prefer, God, wanted to guarantee that there would be procreation. The male was designed to make sure that seed would be planted and life would continue. Men are not naturally monogamous. They were naturally designed to plant their seed everywhere they can. They are the sowers of seed. They are designed to be procreators. Heterosexual males can be sexually stimulated by almost anything that looks or resembles a female. Even color, smell, and sound can sexually excite a man. Sigmund Freud believed that we are all "polymorphous perverse." He believed that many forms of stimulation could sexually arouse people.[127]

The Male Frustration Axiom

So the axiom is this: most males will live with sexual frustration from the time they become sexual until they die. Sexuality has been socialized, and men cannot plant their seed everywhere. In fact, every culture has laws governing sexual practices. There are also social mores that have to be respected and followed or there will be both a personal and a social consequence. Men have to learn how to manage their sexual frustration. If they do not, then they break laws, which can put them in prison, or they violate mores, which will get them divorced. Violation of the social norms can create chaos, disorder, and discord at a level that can ruin a very good relationship. It has the potential to destroy everything that is good and wonderful in a person's life. Men have to learn how to manage their sexual desire and their sexual frustration.

Most men manage their sexual frustration with pornography and masturbation. Here is another axiom: the use of pornography is a normal part of male sexuality. Heterosexual male sexuality is all about feeling attraction to women. It is also about being sexually stimulated by women. That includes real women and also pictures and images of women. Most men are easily sexually excited and hypersensitive to anything sexual. They continually have to deal with sexual frustration throughout their lifetime. I have seen men in my clinical practice who were in their eighties and could not achieve an erection but still felt sexual tension and the desire to have sex. I have known men who had their prostate gland removed because of cancer. They could no longer have erections, yet they still felt sexual tension and the desire to have sexual intercourse. The socialization of the sex drive and the laws of culture do not allow and do limit full sexual expression. Men have to sublimate and masturbate. This is true even when a man is in a very compatible relationship with a woman he loves and with whom he has a satisfying sexual relationship. This may sound like a contradiction, but remember, men never get enough sex. Most women cannot meet a man's sexual needs. Certainly there are exceptions, but I am speaking in general terms. I am referring to averages. I am saying that the majority of married women cannot meet their husbands' sexual needs. It is not so much the quality of the sex as much as it is the quantity of the sex. Men just do not get enough. While a man may love his wife and love having sex with her, he is not monogamous by nature. As the comedian Chris Rock once said in one of his stand-up routines, "A man's fidelity is as good as his options."[128] When a guy is walking around feeling sexual desire and frustration, it is not easy to turn down an opportunity to get relief. It is not that he does not love his wife; it is just that he is biologically designed to plant his seed whenever the opportunity presents itself.

David and Lisa

Let us get back to David and Lisa. There is in Lisa something that is in all women, and there is something in all women that is in Lisa. It is not just the body that attracts men; it is the femaleness that attracts men. If David could not be attracted to other women, then he could not be attracted to Lisa because she is a woman. If he can be attracted to Lisa, then he can be attracted to other women.

Heterosexual men are attracted to many women. Men are biologically designed that way. To be attracted to women and to feel desire to plant their seed is the biological essence of male sexuality. It is the natural purpose of libido. This is primary biology in males—the desire to procreate. Men are designed to become easily aroused. What so many women do not realize is that it is not normal for men to only think of one woman. Men's brains are filled with many female images, even former girlfriends, female fantasies, and sex partners. If the understanding in a marriage is that they are to be sexually exclusive with their partner and maintain a commitment to monogamy, then they must improve their sexual communication, sexual frequency, and emotional connection to keep their commitment. If a couple define commitment to include the male not having thoughts and fantasies of other women, that would create extraordinary hypocrisy from the male because that is impossible for sexually normal males.

Pornography

It is estimated that there are approximately forty-fve million or more Americans who are viewing pornography on computers each month. About 9.4 million are women. This does not include those who are viewing porn in books and magazines. It also does not include those who view porn on cable and satellite television. We know that porn magazine sales total about fifty million dollars a month. Males watch the majority of porn. It is estimated that 72 percent of males and 28 percent of females visit porn websites monthly.[129] Women's pornography often consists of romance novels depicting very explicit and graphic sexual descriptions, which some women find very stimulating. There is also women's porn that is made by women for women.

Only a small percentage of partners who view pornography will cheat on their partner. With so many people viewing sex, it has become a norm. At one time, it was believed that only really "sick" and mentally ill people masturbated. Alfred Kinsey's research disproved that misinformation.

He found that the majority of men masturbated. These were men who were responsible, decent people. They held important positions in the workplace and demonstrated maturity and accountability.[130] I suspect there is currently a lot of negative misinformation about pornography. History may be repeating itself!

The subject of pornography is very difficult and complex. Many people are very critical of the idea of watching porn. There are professional psychologists who condemn porn as being not only destructive of marital relationships, but also as being an addiction that can totally ruin a person's life. The sexual addiction movement continues to gain momentum. It seems that any male getting caught either having affairs or just viewing porn is tagged with the diagnosis of being sexually addicted. Although sexual addiction is a current popular topic and referred to as the new psychological pandemic, many professionals are critical of the idea of sexual addiction. It is interesting to note that the American Psychiatric Association does not recognize Internet addiction or sex addiction as a legitimate category for their fifth edition of the *Diagnostic and Statistical Manual of Mental Disorders*, which will be published in 2013.[131]

The Sexual Addiction Controversy

Dr. Patrick Carnes, PhD, has been promoting sexual addiction and Internet porn as very destructive addictions that are ruining thousands of lives and destroying marriages.[132] He is not alone in his view. Most religions, especially Christian conservatives, Catholics, Mormons, fundamentalists, and some far-to-the-right feminists, do not support any viewing of pornography. However, you should be made aware that these groups also do not support gay rights, gay marriage, comprehensive sex education, contraception, freedom of choice about abortion, the morning-after pill, the right to have sexual autonomy, which would include sex before marriage, and the practice of masturbation. In addition, they consistently have a problem with feminism. It seems that those who are against viewing anything erotic or explicit are also negative about most other sexual issues. For them, sex is dangerous. They support censorship of art, books, movies, and plays.

Criminologists and social workers that study and work with criminals and sex offenders dismiss pornography as a causal factor.[133] They see early childhood experiences, the cultural social structure they come from, brain physiology, and mental illness as the causal factors.[134] Even Dr. Patrick Carnes recognizes that there are established mental health categories that could explain the behavior of many clients he diagnoses as sexually addicted. He states: "During the assessment process, a therapist needs to rule out all other possible diagnoses that may be complicating the clinical presentation. Common ones include: anti-social personality disorder, narcissistic personality disorder, bi-polar disorder, delusional disorder (erotomanic subtype), cognitive disorders, (e.g. brain injury, etc.,) paraphilias, and impulse control disorders. Common co-morbid conditions include substance abuse dependence, eating disorders and ADHD."[135] Would that not almost entirely cover what he wants to diagnose as sexual addiction? What he calls a sexually addicted client could be an antisocial personality disorder or a narcissistic personality disorder.

We know that a small percentage of people have a condition called compulsive sexual behavior. Others have compulsive gambling behavior, or compulsive drinking, or compulsive hoarding or collecting. These unfortunate people ruin their marriages and their lives because they have a mental or psychological disorder. It is not that sex causes addiction and ruins them; they ruin their own lives because of a mental condition they cannot help. They do not even understand it. Carnes describes the extreme cases to make his point, but the behavior he describes is not unlike what happens to the lives of anyone with a personality disorder or a mental illness.[136]

Sexual addictions are talked about in our culture as if they were a pandemic disease spreading throughout society, ruining lives and marriages. However, this is not the situation. To the contrary, this represents a small minority of disturbed or immature people. The rest sounds like hype. There are millions of dollars being made from the sexual addiction movement. The reason there are so many social scientists and professionals who are uncomfortable with this movement is the concern that this sexual addiction crusade is a repeat of history. Remember what was said about masturbation during the nineteenth century? Have we entered into a Neo-Victorian movement in American society? Are the judgments being made about pornography and sex just part of the negative sexual scripting by those who fear sexual freedom and sexual autonomy? Now that science has proven that masturbation is not harmful, is pornography the new target to repathologize? Dr. Marty Klein talks about people whom he calls "erotophobes." These people fear anything erotic as being sinful, harmful, or unhealthy.[137] The erotophobes present themselves as guardians of conventional morality. They have difficulty with sexuality and promote a negative sexual script as the sexual standard for society. They continually exaggerate, distort, misinform, and lie about sexual issues.

The Research on Pornography

When you look at the research on viewing pornography, you can find whatever you are looking to find. The research is confusing because it is so distorted and biased by false research designed to make porn menacing. There is voluminous research that is not research. It is made up to appear to support what the negative sexual script erotophobes have been perpetuating for centuries. They create research with a bias toward supporting their bias! Real research is submitted for peer review in recognized university research journals. In these journals, the research is described, and other research scientists can review how the research data was gathered and how it was interpreted. Other scientists can duplicate the research if they choose. There is always some bias in all research, but some purported research is little more than propaganda.

One well-known example is the research on the effects of pornography commissioned by President Ronald Reagan in 1986. This is often referred to as the Meese Commission Report, since President Reagan had Attorney General Edwin Meese chair the report. This "research" concluded some very negative views on pornography and recommended making it against the law. The Meese Report was rejected by the scientific community on the observation that it was based on politics and not science. It was criticized because it lacked any scientific evidence to support its conclusion.[138]

A recent study on the effect of pornography on men by Dr. Simon Louis Lajeunesse, a researcher at the University of Montreal, Canada, found that all the men in the study supported equal rights for women. Pornography did not change their perception of women. Dr. Lajeunesse made a very poignant observation: "If pornography had the impact that many claim it has, you would just have to show heterosexual films to a homosexual to change his sexual orientation."[139] Other studies have concluded that men who watch pornography compared to men who do not, are more empathic toward women and supportive of women's issues.[140] In other words, they like women!

Let us put aside the research on how harmful viewing pornography may or may not be. Here are some interesting facts that we do know. When we look at other cultures, it is apparent that pornography and violence against women may have no relationship at all. Denmark legalized all pornography in 1967. They had a 68 percent drop in sex crime.[141] Likewise, Japan legalized all pornography in 1972. From 1972 to 1995, there was a drop in rapes from 4,677 per year to 1,500 per year. In the United States, rape has dropped 85 percent since 1973. That is in spite of the obvious increases in access to pornography. Research shows that between 1980 and the year 2000, states that have the greatest Internet access also have the largest decrease of rape per capita. Alaska, Colorado, New Jersey, and Washington, which have the highest rate of access to Internet pornography, also had a 27 percent decrease in rape. The states with the lowest access to Internet porn (Arkansas, Kentucky, Minnesota, and West Virginia) had a 53 percent increase in rape. Remember that nationally rape has dropped by 85 percent, but it has increased where access to Internet porn is limited.[142]

What Is Pornography?

America's Puritan and Victorian history labels almost anything as pornographic. Nudity is pornographic. *Playboy Magazine* shows mostly nude women. There are no penises. It is still condemned as pornographic. In America, those who are fearful of their sexuality define anything that can be sexually arousing as pornographic. They have censored Classic art and rejected books that have sexual content in them. They have banned books from libraries and bookstores. Some of these books are considered classic works. Here are some examples: *An American Tragedy, The Arabian Nights, The Art of Love, Confessions, Fanny Hill, Forever Amber, The Kama Sutra, Lady Chatterley's Lover, Lolita, Madame Bovary, Peyton Place, Tropic of Cancer, Women in Love,* and *Ulysses.*[143]

Americans are not to view anything that is naked or erotic. We are not supposed to see or read anything that has a sexual content. Is there a difference between erotica and pornography? We are not to see sex, read anything that may be erotic, or even fantasize about sex. Essentially, we are not to be aroused by anything other than our spouse. We are to have no outlets for sexual expression other than sex with our married partners. The message is that the sexual arousal is the sin. Most of our states will not even allow comprehensive sex education, out of fear that it will stimulate young adults to have sex before they marry.

This censorship of anything sexual may be explained by that corrupted lust verse (Matthew 5:27–28) in the Bible. We cannot look at nudity, not even if it is art, because it might create lustful thoughts! The fear is that lust is immoral and sinful.

Let me define the different kinds of pornography:

1) erotica (sex) with violence,
2) erotica (sex) with a child or minor,
3) erotica (sex) with an animal,
4) erotica (sex) with abuse and degradation toward women or men (demeaning and degrading, but not violent),
5) nudity (naked men or women but no sex).
6) erotica (sex) between two or more consenting adults with no abuse or degradation.

Number 6 is what most people are watching. If a married couple filmed themselves having sex that would be called pornography in this culture. Could there possibly be some positive benefits to viewing consenting adult, nonviolent, and nondegrading sex?

Some benefits to watching erotic videos are:

1) Watching erotic videos can help desensitize you of sexual inhibitions, guilt, and fear.

Through repeated viewing, it can help you become more comfortable with having sex and with trying different positions and arousing techniques. Women, more than men, have difficulty becoming desensitized to erotica. Some men who come from an orthodox religious background can have difficulty viewing erotica. They have received so many negative messages about being sexual that they are fearful of erotic feelings. They are taught that lust is sinful and wrong.

Women receive considerable social conditioning to guard against ever behaving like a slut and a whore. Of course, some would feel that anyone who would expose their sexuality on a video for everyone to view must be a slut and a whore. You can make love, but you cannot make erotica.

2) Erotic videos can teach you how to make erotica.

It often takes repeated viewing in order to get comfortable with focusing on your own eroticism. Doing so can help you become more comfortable getting into an aroused state, which will ultimately give you more pleasure. If a woman wants to become orgasmic, she needs to learn how to surrender to erotic feelings, just like the men and women in the videos. Porn stars can be excellent models for sexual freedom, because they have completely disinhibited themselves. They are not afraid of deep erotic states. Study how they make erotica. Suspend judging them and, instead, posture as a pupil or student to learn from them. Remember, the desensitizing process is repetitive. You may have to make yourself watch the sex video over and over until you can relax with it and stop judging it. Then you can learn from it. Most people are so negatively scripted that they have a very difficult time seeing anything in pornography that could be positive.

3) Erotic videos can be educational.

Sometimes it is the only source of clear information on how to have good sex. It can demonstrate techniques on how to give and receive pleasure. Visual learning is one of the best sources for comprehension of almost anything. There are studies that conclude that some couples find viewing pornography improved their sex life and their marriage. One study done in Australia surveyed more than one thousand porn users. It found that 90 percent of the viewers believed watching porn made them more attentive to their partners, more accepting of their sexuality, and less judgmental of body shapes. Those surveyed felt that viewing porn actually made their relationships and marriages stronger.[144] Often couples who watch porn together find that they can talk about their sexuality more freely.

4) It can be helpful as a psychological aphrodisiac.

Pornography stimulates the sexual center of the brain, which helps to move a person from everyday reality to erotic reality. Erotic videos can get your mind focused on sex. Erotic videos can be a part of foreplay. It can heighten sexual excitement in preparation for intercourse.

5) It can help in the release of sexual tension.

Erotic videos can be a wonderful sexual partner. They provide the means to have sex with yourself. It can also enrich sexual fantasy. Sexual fantasy induces arousal that moves you into an erotic state. This is helpful for reaching orgasm and releasing all sexual tension. Often a person is feeling some sexual tension that is keeping them from concentrating. They have difficulty focusing or even falling asleep.

Imagine a scale of one to ten, with ten being reaching a climax and one being not feeling sexual at all. When a person is at five or six on the scale, they have enough sexual tension to make them uncomfortable, but not enough tension to be able to relieve themselves from the sexual tension. Pornography can stimulate them to a ten!

Arguments against Pornography

One of the oldest arguments against pornography is that it is sexist; that it makes sex objects out of women. Both men and women are "sports objects," in athletic competition, but nobody complains about that. Look at any magazine rack in the stores and you will see women models on the covers of the most popular magazines. Those models are clearly objects. It is interesting that some of the women who get so upset about making women sex objects in erotic videos buy the magazines on the store rack that make objects of women on their covers. It really is about sex. Both men and women are objects in modeling, advertising, and the fashion industry. In fact, cosmetics, hair styling, and fashionable clothing make objects out of everyone. The first thing we see about a person is the appearance of the person as an object. The real issue for those who protest too much is their own discomfort over women being sexual and surrendering to their own erotic feelings. Has anyone who gets upset with women in porn videos ever considered that there are women who love sexual pleasure and have learned how to enjoy being erotic? Could some of the women in porn films be women who enjoy giving and taking sexual pleasure?

Given the fact that there is a wide variety of pornographic films on the market, everyone needs to choose which films best suit their own needs. You need to find what erotic films you are comfortable viewing. There are erotic films made by amateurs who are not professionals, but a couple, often married, who decided to make a porn film. There are also what is called "women's pornography," which is pornography made by women for women. Some people are critical of erotic films because they think normal women do not do sex the way they are depicted in the porn movie. While that may be true for most women, it is not true for all women. There are women who make love just like the women in the porn movies. For these women, there is very little that bothers them about sexual activity when making love. They are liberated from the negative sexual scripting in our culture. They are part of the 9.4 million women who view and enjoy pornography on their computers. Many more enjoy the sexual stimulation from other sources, like books and magazines.

There is some very credible scientific research supporting the view that sexism and violence against women is not caused by pornography.[145] Those social aberrations against women are caused by social structure not by sex films. The history of killing women as witches was not caused by pornography. Making women cover themselves from head to toe and walk behind the male or being submissive to the male is not caused by pornography. Blaming women for the downfall of all mankind as the descendants of Eve is not caused by pornography. Discriminating against women having positions of authority and power is not caused by pornography.

In the Middle East, women are discriminated against even though pornography is against the law. In some parts of the Middle East, women are not permitted to go to school or learn to read. Honor killings of women and blaming and arresting women when they are raped is not caused by pornography. There is more violence toward women in American movies than you will ever see in pornography. Slasher films, serial killer movies, along with a host of thriller movies in which women are raped, beaten, and killed are not caused by pornography. Many women watch these "violence toward women" movies. They do not seem bothered too much about sexism and violence toward women in the movies, but if it is a porn movie, it becomes a big issue. They are really feeling discomfort with the lust. The negative scripting prevalent in our culture has conditioned them. It seems like violence, killing, and rape are more acceptable in America than lust and sex!

There are movies showing in our theaters that many of us would never care to see. In our local theaters, we pick and chose what we want to see. We should be selective about the erotic films we watch. There is a plethora of distasteful porn that many of us could never enjoy. We have to sort out erotic movies that fit our taste. A couple might consider making their own porn film to watch. The real issue is that in the American culture there does not seem to be any approval of any explicit sex videos or even books that are erotic or sexual in nature. Compared to men, the majority of women in America lack sexual desire and have profound difficulty reaching orgasm. How much of this problem is related to their negative conditioning about sex? The fact that so many married women's sexual interests vary so much from their male counterparts actually contributes to and inspires the male interest in pornography. Wives who lack an interest in sex can also be a contributing factor to male infidelity. It is also probable that if we got rid of all porn there would be an increase in marital infidelity.

There is another contributor to the difference in sexual desire between most men, as compared to most women. Women's bodies produce androgen. The male body also produces androgen. Androgen produces testosterone. Science knows that it is the testosterone in both the female and the male that creates sexual desire. There are minorities of women who produce higher levels of testosterone. These women tend to feel great desire, almost like that of the male. However, the majority of males produce twenty to forty times more the amount of testosterone than the majority of women.[146] This could explain why males desire so much sex and why they have so much sexual frustration. It would also explain why there is such a difference in sexual interest between men and women.

How Men Manage Sexual Frustration

For men, sexual fulfillment comes with having sex with a woman and with having sex with themselves. For most men, pornography is helpful to their reaching fulfillment. Most heterosexual men like looking at women. They also like looking at women having sex. What they find exciting about two women having sex is seeing both women in a sexual state of arousal and looking at their female bodies. A woman's arousal will arouse a man.

Most men find that porn or erotic material helps them with their sexual frustration. Fantasy sex releases sexual tension and gives pleasure. Men often use the erotic state as a great escape. They crawl into porn as if it is a comforting womb that protects them from all the frustrations, threats, and stresses of everyday reality. What would men feel if there was no porn available? Given that most men have pornographic minds, they would manage with their own fantasy world that they would create.

For the minority of men who seem to lack sexual desire, pornography is of little interest to them. They just do not have a strong sexual passion for women. Men who have strong orthodox religious beliefs against pornography and masturbation abstain or participate very little in these erotic experiences. Often those men who make the loudest moral protest are the ones having the most difficulty with it.

Males and Sexual Performance

There are some serious issues for men about performance anxiety. Women can have sex just by "opening the gate." Even if they cannot lubricate, they can use commercial lubricants. For the male, he has to get an erection, but that is not enough. He has to keep that erection for a certain length of time. That is not enough. He also has to be able to release, have an orgasm, and go flaccid. Some men use Viagra, Cialis, or Levitra because they have health conditions that keep them from getting an erection without it. Many men who do not really need erection drugs use them to feel security about having and keeping an erection. While women need a feeling of emotional connection, men are worried about their performance and sexual functioning. Unlike women, most men reach an orgasm almost every time they have sex, but that does not necessarily mean they have performed well with their partners. The majority of men want their partners to enjoy having sex with them. They want it to be pleasurable for her. While women would like to hear, "I love you" after sex, they usually hear, "Did you come?" Men are more focused on how they performed rather than how they feel about their partner.

Men can experience and most often will experience some sexual dysfunction during their lifetime. That is obvious by the large sale of erection medication. Many men still are concerned about the size of their penis. The average male penis is about five inches in length when erect. Some males are as large as seven or eight inches, but not many men have a penis much larger. The diameter of the average penis is approximately one and a half inches to two inches. A woman's vagina can accommodate almost any diameter of penis, but the average woman's vaginal canal is only about four inches long. That means if a man is too long, he can cause pain for the woman if his thrusting causes his penis to bang against her cervix. When this happens, it is like kicking her ovaries. She will feel pain similar to having cramps. A man can have too large a penis for the size of his female partner. If he does, he will have to either shorten his stroke with his partner, have her mount him on top so that she can adjust the stroke, or use the anterior position, which can better accommodate his larger penis. Men can also have difficulty in coming too soon. The average male can stroke for about three to five minutes, and then he will come. The average women needs between eight and ten minutes of stroking to reach satisfaction. This makes for a problem for many couples. Men need to learn how to last longer and women need to learn how to come faster. It is important for couples to spend more time with using foreplay, which will make it easier for the female to come more quickly. Men who come too soon more than 50 percent of the time need to seek sex therapy to remedy the problem. Likewise, men who have difficulty releasing should seek help. Males who are too focused on performance should also seek counseling.

There are really no nerve endings in the vagina that give any sexual feeling.[147] There are some nerve endings that can give some feeling in the first two inches of the vaginal opening right behind the vaginal muscle. If a woman has a G-spot, she can have some erotic feeling in the first inch or two of her vaginal opening. Therefore, penis size really is not that important. If your female partner is attracted to you and likes you, she will be satisfied with your penis. Most men want their female partner to enjoy sex with them. Some men find satisfying their female partner as a large part of their own sexual fulfillment. The great majority of men enjoy pleasure in sex. They have little trouble reaching orgasm.

When males have sexual dysfunction, it is very troubling for them. Being able to perform is more important than being emotionally connected to their partner. Could a woman's need to feel close and connected to her partner be so important because she is not comfortable having sex just for her own erotic pleasure? Does she need some higher purpose or value other than erotica? For males, sex is often about tension release. They feel strong sexual tension, and they feel pleasure when they can release that tension in orgasm. It has been my observation that when men are feeling strong sexual tension, their judgment is often impaired. They have difficulty focusing and concentrating because they feel so horny. They will often think things and do things they would not do if they had not had so much sexual tension. Being in an erotic state is so different from being in a normal everyday state of reality. Nevertheless, most men find great pleasure in sex. Reaching orgasm is not difficult for the majority of men, because they have learned how to surrender to erotica and to enjoy the pleasure of being in an erotic state. There are no books written on how a man can have an orgasm!

The Male Difficulty with Getting Emotionally Connected

For most men, sex is more a physical experience than an emotional one. For most women, sex is more of an emotional experience. They want to feel connected to their male partner. They often complain that sex with their partner feels so mechanical. They say they feel like a prostitute. Because of the way men are culturally conditioned, they often do have difficulty with the expression of their emotions and feelings. It may be that in sex, some of the issues from the nonsexual part of a couple's relationship come to the foreground. If men knew how to make "emotional love" to their partners out of the bedroom, would this feeling of lack of connection in sex exist? Alternatively, if women were more focused on erotica and the sexual sensations of their own body, would emotional connection be such an issue for women?

Chapter Seven:

Marriage: Relating and Dating.

When you read the story of David and Lisa in Chapter 6, what did you feel about them? Did you think their relationship was in serious trouble? Could you see trouble in their future together? Did you think David might eventually have an affair? If so, would you blame it on the pornography that David is watching? Would you blame it on Lisa's negative sexual script? Would you blame David for not being more direct and aggressive in communicating his needs to Lisa? What does Lisa need to become aware of? What is David not aware of? Does Lisa understand that she is setting all the rules for their sexual relationship? Does she understand that she and David are in very different places with sex? Does she realize that the sexual boundaries she has set are so restrictive that they are inspiring David to think more of other women? Does David have any idea that if he is ever given the option he will probably get involved with someone else? Is he aware that he relates to Lisa as if she were his mother? At other times, he wants her for sex as if she is nothing more than a sex object. David has no idea or ability to make "emotional love" to Lisa. He never really connects with her, and on some level she knows that he does not. David and Lisa never fight. If they ever start to fight, they end it very quickly. They end it before either of them can learn anything. David withdraws and becomes quiet. Lisa yells, starts to cry, and runs to the bedroom, slamming the door behind her.

The Elephant in the Living Room

David and Lisa communicate on the surface. They keep their interaction hygienic and banal. They do not talk about what really matters. They both avoid what is uncomfortable and unpleasant. The rule is to always be positive about everything. Both of them think that they have a good marriage. They would both say that they love each other. They might even celebrate the fact that they never fight! Do you see the "elephant in the living room," which they will not talk about?

Any competent marriage counselor, at first meeting, would recognize immediately that this marriage has serious problems. The night Lisa caught David looking at pornography on his computer was a very fortunate event for the health and future of their marriage. This event motivated them to dive deeper into the repressed issues in their relationship. How can David and Lisa have a good marriage when they do not know how to talk to each other? There are no good marriages without good communication. Relevant issues are not going to be addressed if you do not have the skills of communication. Communication requires more than just talking and listening. Communication has to be more than making noise at each other. The basic structure of an interaction between two people is that one talks and the other listens. That may seem simple enough, but when you have emotional issues and are upset, it is difficult to listen. If you are being criticized, you instinctively want to defend yourself. When you hear a couple talk and you hear both their voices talking at the same time, you know that nobody is listening. In communicating, couples need to take turns with listening and talking.

Why does David withdraw from Lisa and depress his self-expression? There are several possibilities. He may not know what to say; he may know what he wants to say but is afraid to say it for fear it will upset Lisa. David may withhold his self-expression because he is angry at Lisa and chooses not to respond to her. He may keep quiet as a form of punishment when he is angry with her. Being unresponsive is often referred to as the "silent treatment."

Another reason why David may not express himself has to do with his fear of intimacy. He fears that if he expresses what he feels, he is making himself a target for Lisa's criticisms and putdowns. He fears she will make him look stupid. What he wants to say may be so personal that he feels embarrassed to say it.

What Couples Need to Learn

One of the first things that David had to learn was that without telling Lisa what he felt, nothing could be worked out. If David did not know what he was feeling then he would need some help from a therapist to learn to identify his feelings. However, in his case, he knew what he felt but was afraid to express it.

One of the first things that Lisa had to learn was that she does not listen to David when he tries to tell her what he feels. Whenever she hears something negative, she exits the transaction, so it cannot be an interaction. Even her crying was a defense against listening to David, because her crying would always stop the communication, especially when her crying was accompanied with anger.

I have heard many women complain that their husbands will not talk to them. What these women often do not recognize is that whenever their husband does try to talk, they cut him off before he can finish a sentence. They are never able to complete their thought before their wife is reacting to it and giving a defensive response. This usually either shuts the husband up or makes him get defensive and dismiss his wife. Then his voice gets louder, and his wife yells at him to stop yelling at her. Women say they want their husbands to talk to them, but often when they do they are cut off before they can complete what they want to say.

Why Men Find It Hard to Listen to Women

Men do not listen to women. I have seen many couples where the husband thinks they are coming in for marriage counseling, when the wife is actually finished with the marriage and wants to talk about divorce. When the wife tells him she is leaving, the husband is always surprised. Although his wife had warned him and told him consistently that she was going to leave, he never heard her or listened. Why could he not hear? So many men in America just do not take women seriously.[148] Countless times I have watched men try to talk their female partner out of her feelings. It usually makes them more angry and defensive or, worse yet, they just get quiet and stop talking. If women are supposed to be submissive to men, then why should men listen to them? According to the Bible, wives are supposed to submit to what their husbands say.

Remember, this is a patriarchal culture. Some of the Bible verses quoted in chapter two teach that a woman "shall have no authority over a man," and that women should "keep silent." Women should defer all decisions to their husbands.

Sweden has the most equality between men and women. Women earn the same pay as men in most occupations in Sweden. In addition, they have the same balance of men and women in almost all occupations.[149] Sweden treats prostitutes very humanely. The government does not arrest them. The government provides funding for them to be retrained for a different career if they want to discontinue prostitution.[150] This is not true in America, where the Puritan-Victorian distrust of women and the support of patriarchy still rules.

The Catholic Church claims to support women's rights and women's equality, but have you ever seen a female Catholic priest, bishop, cardinal, or pope? Have you ever compared a nun's status with the power and status of the males who administrate and control everything in the Church? Those who promote the negative sexual script think of women as the weaker gender. Women cannot really be trusted to hold the highest office in America. Unlike most of the countries in the world, America has never elected a female president. What countries have been able to elect a female as president or prime minister? Here are just a few: England, India, Portugal, Bolivia, Israel, Iceland, Norway, Holland, the Philippines, Yugoslavia, Central African Republic, Finland, Panama, Mongolia, Bermuda, Switzerland, Ireland, Canada, France, Nicaragua, Pakistan, Germany, New Zealand, Poland, and Malta.[151] This is not the exhaustive list. Besides the empowering of women in governmental positions, the business world is also illustrative of denying women power. In America, among the top Fortune 500 companies, women hold only approximately 20 percent of the upper management positions.[152]

How We Treat Women Prostitutes

While we are looking at our cultural attitudes toward women, consider how we treat female prostitutes. Prostitution is against the law everywhere in America, except in Nevada. In all the other forty-nine states, prostitutes are arrested, fined, and even jailed. They are treated with complete contempt. Most Americans are not aware of all the countries in the world where prostitution is not only legal, but where it is also against the law to be a pimp. In many other countries, pimps are arrested, but not the prostitutes. Among those countries are: Brazil, Bulgaria, Canada, Finland, France, Germany, Greece, Israel, and Sweden.[153] These countries do not punish women as if they were Eve. We do in America. In many countries, being a prostitute or a pimp is legal. Some of those countries include: Costa Rica, the Czech Republic, Denmark, Hungary, Italy, Kenya, Mexico, Holland, New Zealand, Norway, Romania, Spain, Switzerland, England,

Russia, Singapore, Austria, and Australia.[154] It is not that these countries with legalized prostitution do not have any morality. They recognize that most women are in prostitution to keep from being economically impoverished. They do not treat them as if they were Eve! America is still a very patriarchal culture. Women are still discriminated against. They are disparaged by men. Their feelings and opinions are still discounted. We still have the double standard. Men can be sexually active and somehow it makes them manly. When women are sexually active, they are often referred to as sluts and whores. Some men feel they do not have to respect women. They feel justified in discriminating against them. They can feel comfortable exploiting and using women, because they view them as the weaker sex. Men often discount what women feel, because males think they are irrational.

There are certainly exceptions, but generally, husbands have difficulty listening to their wives and accepting what they are saying. There is another factor that contributes to men having difficulty listening to women. As little boys, they grew up with a mother who was obviously female. Our mothers did most of the caretaking and parenting when we were boys. Usually our mothers called us to come in to take a nap or to wash up for dinner. Our mothers did almost everything for us. They did our laundry, changed our sheets, made our bed, fed us, advised us, warned us, told us what we could and could not do. Most males heard their mother's voice more than any other person's voice while they were growing up. That is why we built up immunity to listening to our mothers. We were playing with peers, having so much fun, when we heard mother calling us to get home. We pretended like we did not hear her or we ran and hid from her. When she caught up with us, she was angry and scolded us. By the time, we were teens, we stopped listening to her fears, worries, and warnings. A few years later, when we married a woman, we unconsciously slipped into the same psychological posture that we formed with our mothers. Men often feel that women worry too much, whine too much, get too emotional and irrational. Then there are all the stories of women and their monthly periods that make them so irrational. Therefore, husbands stop listening, and when they do listen, they do not take anything their wife says seriously. In fact, they discount whatever their wife says, simply because it is coming from a woman. That connection between mother and wife is close enough to tune out the wife as if she were the mother. John Gottman's research verifies that men who do not allow their wives' feelings and opinions to influence them have higher levels of marital dissatisfaction.[155]

Learning to Communicate Effectively

What have David and Lisa learned from their marriage counselor? They learned that when they are going to talk about their relationship issues, they have to agree that they will follow some important rules.

1. They should set a time and time limit to their conversation. When the time runs out, they should renegotiate the time.
2. They have to agree that no one exits from the conversation and runs from the interaction.
3. They agree to take turns listening and talking. No one talks at the same time as the other. If one of them cuts the other off before they are finished, the one being cut off should tell the other to "let me finish; you are cutting me off." They should not proceed further until the person who was talking regains the floor. Cutting your partner off will create defensiveness. It usually takes the form of your partner cutting you off in return.
4. They should not attack their partner's self-esteem. No labeling or name-calling is allowed. David does not call Lisa a "bitch," and Lisa does not call David an "asshole" or a "prick."
5. They must make "I" statements to each other, rather than "you" statements. When one makes "you" statements, such as "you always think negatively about what I do," it creates defensiveness. It sounds parental. It sounds as if you are the authority on the other person, you are right, and you have the truth. To the contrary, it is more helpful stating, "I feel that you think negatively about what I do." That allows the possibility that you may be wrong. It is simply how you feel; you are not stating that this is definitely how it is. It is just how you feel, but your feelings could change if your partner shows you how your feelings are not accurate. All feelings are valid for the person who feels them. Lisa could complain, "I feel that you are too critical of me." David previously responded defensively, "I don't think that is true at all." What he learned subsequently in his therapy is that there must be some validity to Lisa's feelings or she would not have them. He has learned to listen to what she is saying and not to invalidate what she says are her feelings.

Addressing the Issues that Matter

So now that we have David and Lisa understanding how to communicate, what are the issues that they need to address? Lisa wants to talk about the lack of connection she feels with David. She feels that most of the time he is preoccupied. She feels that he does not tell her what he feels or even what is on his mind. She has observed that when a friend of his calls him on the phone, he talks with a real spontaneity that he never does with her. She feels he never tells her that he loves her unless she says it first, and then it does not sound like he really means it. Although she does almost all the cooking and cleaning, she never feels that David appreciates what she does. She works in the marketplace, and she works in their home. She does his laundry, folds it, and puts it in his drawer. Almost anything he asks her to do for him, she does willingly. She rarely receives a thank-you. She wants him to do more around the house. She feels that they really do not do anything together. When they do, she feels that she must always be the one to initiate it. While she is reporting this, she is holding back her tears. It is obvious that when she thinks about how David treats her, she is unhappy and lonely in her marriage to him.

It is easy to guess what David wants to address: sex! David is like the majority of men. Sex is one of the most important issues in his life. It is important because he desires it so much and because he feels so much sexual frustration. He is attracted to Lisa's body and likes having sex with her, but what he does not like is her inhibition and the control that she maintains throughout their sexual experience. She dictates what they can and cannot do. She also gets to determine when and where they will have sex. David does not believe she really has orgasms. After having sex with her, he always asks her if she came or not. He says it never seems like she ever lets go and comes. Lisa always says that she does, but David never believes her.

Becoming a More Erotic Woman

Lisa's marriage counselor recommended that she read Dr. Lonnie Barbach's excellent book, *For Yourself*. [156] This is probably one of the best books ever written for women on the subject of masturbation. It was written for women to help them become desensitized to the negative sexual script that condemns having sex with one's self. Once a woman has worked through the negative messages about masturbation, she can gain all the benefits discussed in chapter five. After some needed education about reaching orgasm, Lisa came for the first time.

Lisa started a completely new sex life with herself. It became a new meaning in her life to experience this pleasure and enjoyment. She was learning how to enjoy her body. She was giving herself a private pleasure that had a surprising affect on her. She started to like her body more, and with that discovery, she started liking herself more. She would tell David, "I like me, and I like my body." She now realized how enjoyable her body was to her. Her spirit and her body developed a new friendship through her acceptance and approval of masturbation. As she continued to stimulate herself and reach orgasm, other things began to happen. She started to change the way she dressed. Lisa had previously dressed like a "plain Jane." Now she started to dress more sensually: a touch more cosmetics, a bit more jewelry, clothes that fit a bit tighter, a different bra that didn't try to hide her breasts, and shoes that had a touch of sensuality. She became more conscious of feeling sensuous. For the first time in her life, she felt in touch with her sexuality. The mind was connected to the body; her body connected to her mind. She did more. She started reading books that clearly were erotic in nature. First, she started with the classics that had been banned by the negative sexual script promoters. She read *Lady Chatterley's Lover* and then she read *Lolita*. She found erotic literature stimulating. She was developing a sexual fantasy life, which was helping her in her sexual relationship with herself. It was also helping her in her sexual relationship with David. She went to a store and rented some pornography films. She asked David to make a recording of the kinds of erotic scenes that she found stimulating. This became a custom film of her own with the kind of erotica that helped turn her on. By just copying what appealed to her, she could skip the boring material. She went online and discovered that there was pornography for women. She found porn movies made by women for women.

Lisa fully owned her sexuality. She was integrating her sexuality with her mind and her body. She started risking the use of erotic language. Use of erotic language was a risk because she was always following the script that "good girls don't talk like that." She started to challenge all those negative messages she had been told. Once when starting to make love with David, she said, "Fuck me." Then she said, "Let me feel your cock." Then she said, "Put your cock in me and make my cunt feel good." She realized how the use of erotic language was freeing her. She could move her body more freely as she let go of the negative scripting and surrendered to her lustful feelings. As she focused on her sexual sensations, she found herself moving her body to increase the erotic feeling.

As she fell increasingly into the erotic state she had often experienced in masturbation with herself, Lisa began to move her hips and pelvis in rhythm to David's stroking in her cunt. She was not having sex; she was fucking! She was not making love; she was screwing David! She was making erotica. She felt her passion increase to a place where she was hardly conscious of David, because the sexual tension she was creating was totally taking over. She could only feel profound sexual tension and then a flood of pleasure that seemed to weld her mind and body together. She could feel pelvic contractions, which were involuntary. With each contraction, she felt a surge of pleasure and a release of all tension. She felt so good. She was now able to return to David who had also released just after she had. She enjoyed herself so much. She felt a deep love for David for participating in her pleasure. She said to him softly, "I just love fucking you." David did not have to ask her if she had come. He felt her contractions and he had heard her moans of pleasure. All David said was, "God, I love you!" They held each other very tightly.

The Monogamous Slut-Whore Pleasure

As their sex life improved, David found his interest in pornography declining. He had never felt so turned on to Lisa as he was now. Often they would view twenty minutes of porn, just to help them shift from everyday reality to erotic reality. Sometimes when Lisa was not available, David would watch some porn and have sex with himself. Sometimes when David was not available, Lisa would watch some porn and have sex with herself. Lisa had lost her fear of being an erotic woman. She had come to the realization that she had become a whore. She was a slut. If a woman who is a slut and a whore is a woman who enjoys having sex and is sexually active, then Lisa is a slut and a whore. If it also means that she has sex with lots of men, then Lisa is what I would call a monogamous slut and whore, because she is monogamous with David. When some hostile male calls a woman a whore, instead of being offended by that ancient Victorian label, why not just answer back, "And you are such an uptight, hostile prude; no whore would fuck you!" Remember, there is in David what is in all men, and there is in all men what is in David. If Lisa can be turned on to David, then she can be turned on to other men. If she could not be turned on to other men, she could not be turned on to David because he is a man. The core of her attraction is to maleness. She is also polymorphous-perverse. She can be turned on by other men. She is also turned on by music and art. She can be turned on by nature and soft candlelight. She has integrity. She keeps her commitments. No matter how she is aroused, she has committed herself to fulfill all her sexual feelings with herself or with David. She is a monogamous slut and whore. Lisa is not afraid of those words anymore. She is not ashamed that she is sexual. In fact, she feels good knowing she has so much "pussy power." Her sexuality empowered her like she had never known. Fear and inhibition had declined. She was now in control of her sexuality. She had never loved herself more. She had never felt so free to be herself. She could feel her power and confidence as a female who had integrated her body with her mind. Lisa now had her "MSW," and she found those words utterly laughable.

Dating and Relating

After David and Lisa got married, they stopped dating. Couples should never stop dating, no matter how busy they become. In fact, many of the things they did in their courtship should have been carried into their marriage. They had fun when they were courting. Every week was full of dates. They made time to be with each other. Many of the things they did in their courtship should have been carried into their marriage. They hiked beautiful trails, biked for miles, visited the zoo regularly, fished, went to concerts, met for picnics in the park, gave parties and they went to parties, went swimming, went to movies, and took trips. They were constantly planning dates with each other.

Now they have been married for five years, and they do very little together. David was the one who did not want to go anywhere. He always complained that he was too tired from work to do anything. Once a week, he would have beers with some male friends. Most of the time when he was at home, he would just sit and watch sports on television. David never realized how non-intimate he was with Lisa. He had to face some of the dark truth about himself. He did not even think of doing anything to inspire Lisa to want to open the gate and have sex with him. He knew how to make love to her sexually, but he had no idea how to make love to her emotionally. Most of the time, he never really looked at her. He never really studied who she was as a person and a life partner. He did not know the color of her eyes. He did not know her favorite food or her favorite music.

He hardly knew anything about what she suffered as a child. He had no idea about what would make Lisa happy or excited.

David had also forgotten much of what he did know, like the fact that Lisa enjoyed dancing. They had actually met at a dance, but they had not been dancing in the last five years since they had married.

An example of David's lack of relating to Lisa was demonstrated on her last birthday. David bought her flowers, a genuine pearl necklace, some expensive perfume, and a nice card that was signed, "Love you, David." When he gave the gifts to Lisa, she looked at it all and became very solemn. She started to cry; she threw the flowers at him, followed by the pearls and the perfume. She then screamed at him, "For the past year, I have been asking you to build some bookshelves in the basement for my books, and you kept telling me that we couldn't afford the building materials. I do not want pearls and perfume. I have been telling you I wanted you to make me some bookshelves!" She then ran down the hall, went into the bedroom, slammed the door, threw herself on the bed, and sobbed.

If David had been listening to Lisa, if he had been tuned into her, he would have built her some bookshelves for her birthday. Because she felt David never listened to her, she reacted emotionally. She knew that he still did not know who she was after five years together. It was like the last straw. She sobbed in hurt and frustration.

Men Need to Learn About Connecting

David had much to discover in his counseling. He learned that he needed to get to know who he was living with. He could start this process by forgetting about getting her to have sex with him. Instead, he learned to watch what she did when she was home. He started to listen in on her conversations on the phone; he paid attention to how she would meet and greet people. He started to get interested in what she felt about things such as her family, friends, the news in the paper and on television; how she felt about him and their relationship. When she was quiet, he started asking her what she was thinking. He established contact time with her. Contact time involves setting dates to be alone together. It can be as simple as having coffee together, a glass of wine on the patio, or playing board games together ritually, like cards or dominoes. Board games can be relaxing and create an opportunity for chitchat, which can lead a couple to discuss deeper, more meaningful needs. Couples need ritualized contact time in which they get together at the same time almost every day of the week, such as going to lunch once a week, having coffee together every morning, or watching a television program they both like. It is most important to make time daily to sit and talk together about how they are feeling about their relationship. It can be just before they go to bed. It can be while they are in bed. It can be as soon as they are together after work. Contact rituals are absolutely one of the most important components of having a close and emotionally intimate relationship.

The Process of Connecting and Disconnecting

In all relationships, there is a constant connecting and disconnecting process. We may fall asleep feeling close to our partner, but even sleep separates us, so that in the morning we wake disconnected. If you have coffee together with conversation, you may then be reconnected. If there is no time for that, even a genuine kiss and a felt hug can give you a sense of connection. When you both leave to go to work, you are disconnected. If you should call or text your partner and you talk together for a moment, you are connected again. When you return home and have no connecting ritual, then you remain disconnected, maybe even for the entire evening. Couples need to become aware of the continual process of connecting and disconnecting that is always operating in their relationship. My observation is that men would have more sex with partners if they paid attention to more than just the sexual connection. They need to spend more time on the emotional and psychological connections. That is what David learned to do. Your partner is a sex object, but not just a sex object. Your partner is a person like you. Your partner has feelings about many issues in life. When you get to know your partner, you will be connected emotionally and psychologically. When that happens, it is impossible for a third party to get between you and your partner.

As David began to understand this and started to focus on getting to know who Lisa really was as a person, he started to realize how much he was enjoying the relationship. They were actually becoming friends. He started looking forward to seeing her when he came home from work. She felt the change in David. She could tell he was actually listening to her and interested in what she had to say. He was not judging her feelings nor undermining her opinions on issues. She could see that David liked talking to her. He liked listening to her. She actually started to feel that David loved her. It meant a lot to her when David finally built those bookshelves. It made her want to open the gate and open it wide.

Always Having Your Partner with You

When a couple is emotionally, psychologically, and spiritually connected, they feel their partner's spirit inside their own psyche. Even when you are apart, you can feel your connection to your partner. When Lisa is away from David, she feels his spirit, and when David is away from Lisa, he feels her spirit. They are connected in a way that makes it impossible for another person to get in between them. Even though Lisa and David can feel attraction to someone else, they cannot act on that attraction, because they feel as if their mate was standing right there with them. When you feel that emotional connection it is like your partner is always with you. Your partner spiritually is never completely out of your feelings. You can be aware that you are attracted to someone else, but you cannot respond to that someone because you can feel the love you have for the person to whom you have committed your life. You can also feel your partner's love for you. It is nearly impossible to act on some physical attraction when you feel in love with your partner and are aware that your partner is in love with you. You would have to be a masochist, a narcissist, or a sociopath to mess up what is essentially a very good relationship.

David started spending more time with Lisa. She became his closest friend and lover. During sex, he learned to take more time with foreplay. He learned not to move too fast. He took more time to arouse Lisa. He discovered what Masters and Johnson had learned in their sexual research with couples: that if men who have difficulty getting a firm erection learn to stimulate their partners more and focus on their partners' arousal and excitement, they would involuntarily get erect. When men look at porn, they focus on sexual excitement and arousal. They do not have to try and think an erection. They look at the sexual arousal of the woman in the porn and involuntarily get an erection. Now that Lisa knows how to get erotically aroused, and David has learned to take time to focus on arousing her and to concentrate on her arousal, he doesn't have to worry about whether he will get erect or not.

David and Lisa have learned how to communicate; they have learned how to talk and listen; they have learned to suspend judgment on what their partner feels. They now date all the time. Their dating is actually a connecting ritual. No, they do not have to leave the house to go on a date. A connecting date can be on their patio, in their living room, or in their bed. They have learned how wonderful love is before sex and how wonderful it is after sex, but they know the term "making love" is really a cover-up for making erotica together for their pleasure. David and Lisa are no longer controlled by all those authorities, ministers, priests, and institutions that keep reinforcing the negative sexual script. They are enlightened and liberated. That elephant in their living room is gone.

Chapter Eight:

Romantic Marriage: Loving Each Other

Tom and Jackie have been married for thirty-one years. They have two adult children who no longer live with them. In the thirty-one years they have been married, they have never done anything to profoundly hurt each other. There has never been any infidelity. There has never been a level of selfishness so great that it seriously scarred the relationship. Although they had some heavy fighting early in the relationship, they no longer really fight. They have differences from time to time, but they routinely discuss them and negotiate a settlement. There are times when they get emotional when discussing an issue that they disagree on, but after expressing how they feel, they come together like they were on the same team and negotiate an agreement. Their sexual relationship averages around twice a week, sometimes more and sometimes less. They plan dates every day. More than 90 percent of the time, they feel good with each other. The love and attraction they both had in the beginning of the relationship is still felt.

Maintaining the Original Feeling You Had in Courtship

How have Tom and Jackie been able to keep the positive attraction for each other for thirty-one years? If you study their relationship, you will observe how they have managed to do it.

They both have a lot of independence in their relationship. They do many things separately. Tom loves golf and plays weekly with some male friends. Jackie is not interested in golf, but she loves to walk, hike, and bike. She also loves to sew. Tom loves to watch sports on television. Jackie has women friends with whom she likes to go for coffee and she will often walk, talk, and bike with them.

Since they both have careers, they have three bank accounts. One is Jackie's, one is Tom's, and one is a joint account to which they both contribute in order to cover the joint costs of living. It is rare that they ever have an argument about money. Any major purchase they discuss and both contribute their share. From just what I have described about them, can you identify some of the positive characteristics of their relationship?

They both allow each other independence socially, psychologically, and financially. No one is dominant. Tom is not the "head" of the household. There have always been two heads of the household. They have managed to maintain a peer relationship for thirty-one years! Jackie does not feel controlled by Tom, and Tom does not feel controlled by Jackie. It was not like that in the beginning of their relationship. For the first five years of their marriage, they had horrendous fights. They were both strong, independent people. Tom was raised on the teachings of the negative sexual script. In his family, his father was the head of the household. In Jackie's family, her mother was the head of the household. Tom came from a traditional patriarchal family and Jackie from a matriarchal family. They fought for control. They fought to prove who was right. It is difficult for couples to realize that "a fight to be right" is a dead-end fight. There are no winners. If one of you thinks you won, consider that whoever loses gets very resentful toward the partner who won. When a husband keeps losing to his wife, he will usually withdraw and stop talking to her. When a wife keeps losing to her husband, the first thing she usually does is to stop having sex with her husband. It is almost impossible for a woman to have sex with someone toward whom she feels anger and resentment.

Tom and Jackie eventually came to the realization that there were no winners with their fights. Their fighting did not resolve anything. Their fights just made them mad at each other and left them alienated. They discovered that they were both right. In their fights, each of them had a piece of what was true! Neither of them would listen to the other's truth. Each of them would become fixated on their own truth, and they could not hear the truth in their partner's view. They started to really listen to each other with the purpose of understanding how their partner felt, rather than trying to convince their partner they were right and their partner was wrong.

Another observation you may have identified is the fact that they know the rules of good communication and they follow them. When one is talking, the other listens. Listening does not just mean keeping quiet. Listening is an active process of focusing on what your partner is saying and not thinking about what you want to say. You try to put your feet in your partner's shoes. Good listening involves empathy for what your partner is feeling and telling you. If your partner is telling you something that sounds critical, consider that there may be some truth in what your partner is saying.

Tom and Jackie have a very good sex life. It is really above average for their ages and life stage. It is, of course, not frequent enough for Tom, but he compensates by having sex with himself. Sex is frequent enough that he does not feel like he is always being rejected. It is clear to him that Jackie likes sex and is a very sexual, sensual partner. He knows that she is a very erotic woman who likes to have sex, not just to please him, but to pleasure herself. Tom has learned how important foreplay is to Jackie. He takes plenty of time to make sure she is very turned on before they start intercourse. He has paid attention to how she likes to be pleasured. He has listened to what she has told him she likes. Usually, Jackie comes without much effort.

Keeping Yourself and Your Relationship Erotic

Jackie discovered masturbation when she was about twelve years old. She found her clitoris and massaged it regularly. Pleasuring herself to orgasm became a regular activity. It made her feel so good. It relaxed her. It connected her mind to her body. Masturbation gave her a positive feeling about her body. She had her first sexual experience with a boy when she was about sixteen years old. Her mother had told her about birth control and sent her to a class at Planned Parenthood. She knew the importance of protecting herself. Her mother made certain Jackie had easy access to several methods of birth control. Her mother did not teach her abstinence until marriage. Her mother taught her responsibility.

By the time she met Tom, Jackie was very experienced with her sexuality. She knew her body well and she knew how to shift into erotic reality. Orgasm was never difficult for her. She has always enjoyed sex with Tom. Sometimes she will have sex with him just because she knows how important it is to him. Jackie knows how strong the sex drive is in males and has empathy for Tom's sexual frustrations. When she is just trying to please Tom, she often will not have an orgasm, even though he gets satisfied. Although she does not have an orgasm during these encounters, she still enjoys the physical closeness and the giving of pleasure to Tom. Jackie still enjoys masturbation. It is a real part of her sexual enjoyment and her feeling of closeness to herself. Jackie likes feeling sensual. She dresses sensually and is comfortable talking about sex. Sometimes she enjoys sexually teasing Tom. She knows it turns him on. She has no shame about her body and she lets Tom see her nude as much as she is able. She delights in knowing the power of her pussy.

Jackie loves being a woman. She enjoys being a sensual, sexual woman. Knowing this, gives her an erotic spirit that transcends what she weighs or the size of her breasts. Jackie knows she has something far more attractive than a perfect body. Sometimes when she is dressing, if Tom is in the room or comes into the room, she will flash a quick sexual pose at him. Sometimes when Tom comes home and she is sitting in a chair reading, she will lift up her skirt and spread her legs, and then quickly go back to reading. She usually gets a hot kiss from Tom, and just like that they are connected emotionally. It is like she sends him a message that "tonight is the night, but not right now. Let's talk."

Sometimes when Tom is watching pornography, Jackie will look over his shoulder and make comments on how hot and sexy the women look and how the men are great studs. She will often tongue his ear or reach down into his crouch to feel his hard-on. When they are out in public, if they come upon a strikingly beautiful woman, Jackie will point her out to Tom. She might say something like, "Look at her, Tom; isn't she beautiful?" Other times she might say, "Look at her; isn't she hot?"

For Tom, just knowing that Jackie enjoys sex and that he enjoys having sex with her seems to lessen his sexual frustration. Although he does not get all the sex he would like, the quality of the sex he has with Jackie compensates for the lack of quantity of sex. He knows that sex is good and that fact curbs his interest in both pornography and other women he meets in the market place.

The Importance of Date Planning

Tom and Jackie are always planning dates together. A date for them is arranging any contact time for them to do something together. They may make a date to watch the NBA playoffs on Thursday night together. They may make a date to meet on the patio at 8:00 pm for a glass of wine together. They make dates for a concert or a movie. They will make a date to play cards together. For them, dating is planning time to be together. It does not have to be going out, but occasionally they do go out. Most often, it is stopping what they are doing independently and coming together. What is so important is that they are planning contact time every day. It is always something they are going to do together. Most of the time, they make dates just to talk. Sometimes they have spontaneous dates, where the one comes to the other and says, "Let's take a break together." Then they drop what they are independently doing and come together. Sometimes they make dates in the future for trips or concerts and put these dates on their calendars. Often during the week, they plan what they are going to be doing on the weekend. What is very clear is that Tom and Jackie have made their relationship a priority. Getting together for contact time is what is primary in their lives. There is not a day of the week that they do not talk to each other.

The Language of Endearment

There is something else that explains the close connection of Tom and Jackie. In the early years of their marriage when they were having what seemed like constant power struggles, they went to a marriage counselor. The counselor taught them something that made a truly remarkable difference in their relationship. In fact, couples that learn what they have learned will feel an emotional intimacy the likes of which they have never known.

Have you ever considered that emotional intimacy has its own language? If you learn this language and use it in your communication, you will feel a closer bond. What is this language? I have called it the language of endearment. The exchange of endearing language between a couple creates a warm, intimate feeling in their relationship. Endearing language is romantic language. It is the language of poets and lovers. If you focus on all the right features of your partner—the personal qualities you saw when you first met, the qualities of your partner that you still appreciate—and you start to verbalize that information to your partner, you will be endearing your partner. If your partner will reciprocate so that it is a mutual exchange, then you will be making emotional love to each other. It will create a feeling of closeness. What makes the language of endearment so powerful is the fact that it is a form of emotional reinforcement. Couples need to learn this form of reinforcement in their relationship. Couples who do this have a feeling of connectedness that is almost impossible for someone else to break. Let me illustrate.

Tom and Jackie are sitting in their living room reading on a Saturday morning.

Jackie: "Tom, I just love being with you like this. Isn't it nice just to be so relaxed together reading?"

Tom: "Yeah, this is really nice. I just love being with you."

Jackie: "I feel so lucky to have someone like you in my life."

Tom: "I really love you. I can't imagine being happier with anyone else."

Jackie: "You are such a love. Where did I ever find you? I am so lucky to have a man like you."

Tom: "I feel I am so lucky to have a woman like you. I have never met anyone like you. You are so responsible and loving to me. I really appreciate all that you do for me and for us."

Jackie: "You've been such a great father to our kids. You are just a lot of fun. I really have fun with you. You just make me laugh so much. I think I am so blessed to have someone so wonderful in my life."

Tom: "You are so beautiful. I am so attracted to you. I cannot imagine a better sexual partner than you. I do not know what I would do without you. I am nuts about you. You are the only woman in the world I ever want to be with. I just love you so much."

Jackie gets up out of her chair and goes to Tom: "I just want to hug you."

They hug and kiss, Tom fondles her, and they hold each other for a minute. Then Jackie speaks.

Jackie: "Do you want to make love?"

The language of endearment is always complimentary language. Whatever you say when making emotional love to each other, it is always a validation of the relationship and your partner. The focus is totally on what is right about your partner and your relationship together. You never mention any negatives when you are being endearing. The interaction between you and your partner should always be positive when you are making emotional love to each other.

Tom: "That was such a great dinner you made last night. I am so lucky to be married to a chef!"

Jackie: "You are such a dear; I am so lucky to have a man like you for a partner. Where did I ever find you?"

Tom: "I think it was under a rock. Jackie, I just love you so much. You are really something else. You are just incredible. I am married to a great person. You are the light of my life. You make my life wonderful."

Romancing Is a Celebration of Your Partner

Couples can use their own creativity to find ways of validating and affirming their partner. Whatever you say does not have to be rational or logical. Remember, the language of endearment is not science; it is poetry. Poets have a license to say things that in fact are not true. A poet can say, "The clouds laughed, the trees danced, and the grass smiled." We all know clouds do not laugh, trees do not dance, and grass does not smile. Such talk does communicate some kind of celebration of nature. It communicates a joyful celebration. It communicates a state of happiness. So when you are making emotional love to your partner, remember it is about poetry, not logic and reason. So Jackie could say to Tom, "I don't want to live without you." In fact, such a statement is not true. If Tom died, Jackie would no doubt fall in love with some other man, rebuild her life, and continue living. That is not the point. Jackie is being a poet. She is expressing how deeply in love she is with Tom and how connected she feels to him. She is affirming how much he means to her. Tom tells Jackie, "Being with you is like being in heaven. When I am with you, the stars shine brighter, my heart wants to dance, and I just feel so good being with you." As a poet, you have a license to exaggerate and embellish with your language to convey your feelings toward your partner. If you looked rationally and objectively at your partner, you would have to think of the negatives that you find frustrating or difficult. That is why you can be less than rational while making emotion/psychological love to your partner.

Expressing compliments to each other reinforces a positive reciprocal feeling in the relationship. Couples need to continue to poetically vow their love for each other through complimentary responses. It is important for couples to take advantage of every opportunity to positively reinforce their relationship. There should be compliments and "I love you" everyday. Every fight or negotiation of a difference should end with the use of endearing language and positive reinforcement of their feelings for each other. Couples who cannot engage in this process need some work on their relationship. If they cannot, then their relationship is emotionally handicapped.

Women seem to be able to do this much easier than most men. So many men are taught that soft emotion is weakness and that real men are never weak. Although men are not called sluts or whores, they are called sissy, pussy, chicken, chicken shit, yellow, yellow belly, weakling, coward, yellow bellied coward, and candy ass. Any tears a boy may have around his peers will name him a cry baby. Men are not supposed to ever be needy or show vulnerability or weakness. Posturing as strong and in control often covers up a man's softness and sensitivity. It also teaches him to repress any feelings that could be judged as weaknesses. Feelings of fear, insecurity, and anxiety are kept hidden for fear he will look weak and unmanly. Remember, men never ask for directions! To do so would be admitting a weakness. They have to be logical and self-contained to appear as if they are in command. This male condition is part of the negative sexual script's definition of a man. It is part of the gender role stereotype for males, to be strong and in control.

Removing Your Mask

We all wear a social mask. There is what is referred to as the "public self" and the "private self." The public self is the mask we wear in public. We present ourselves as feeling good and doing well. We hide the more private feelings of not doing so well and not feeling so good. We are all taught how to conduct ourselves in public. We are polite, respectful, helpful, and generally a nice person who has no problems or worries. The public self has no financial, health, or personal problems. We are taught to put on the happy face in public and hide our true personal and private feelings from public view. When couples meet, they usually present the public self because they want to make a good impression. They want to be liked and loved. If the courtship isn't too long, the private self often will not be revealed in its entirety until a couple has locked into living together or marrying. Real emotional intimacy happens when the private selves meet. Again, it seems that it is easier for most women to reveal their private self than it is for most men. So many men feel that what makes them loveable is the appearance of being strong, powerful, and in control. They fear if they show any weakness they will not be loved by a woman. What so many men do not understand is that hard feelings protect, but soft feelings connect. In emotional intimacy, it is important to let the soft emotion have expression. Letting your sensitivity be expressed creates a feeling of closeness and connection.

When using endearing language with your partner, you are letting out the sensitive, poetic, and romantic dimension of yourself. Couples who learn to do this with each other will develop a very close love bond. The emotion or feeling that endearing language creates is soft, warm, and empathic. You are making psychological love to each other. At first it may feel awkward and uncomfortable. If you continue to express the language of love and endearment, you will not only get comfortable with the language, but you will find that you really do feel the words you are saying. Redundancy is what is most important. You cannot learn any new behavior without repetition. By repeating this process over and over, you not only establish a very positive pattern in your relationship, you establish emotional intimacy.

Keeping Music, Poetry, and Theater in Your Marriage

Imagine that a dictator took over our culture and made it against the law to have music. All forms of music were destroyed. Anyone caught listening or playing music would be executed. Art and drama were also eliminated. Can you imagine what life would be without art? Without music? Without the theater? Music, art, and theater are what inspires our life spirit. They can lift us out of the monotony of the routine to transcendent levels of inspiration and peak experience. Romance is the music in any love relationship. When couples stop romancing each other, they have stopped the music, removed the art, and closed the theater in their relationship. Couples need to learn how to romance each other. They need to open their hearts to each other. By sharing their innermost self, they will create a deep level of emotional love.

Language of endearment is what you express when you are getting along really well and feeling good about each other. It is a way of telling each other that you feel good that you are together. The focus should be on what your partner does right, what you love and appreciate about your partner, what you find satisfying in the relationship. It is all about positive messages being exchanged with each other. Couples need to reinforce the positive qualities in their partners. Positive reinforcement, created by the process of romancing each other, and the use of both the dating and endearment processes are what will strengthen the relationship and secure your marriage.

Infidelity and Monogamy

The majority of marriages in America are monogamous. The National Health and Social Life Survey found that 25 percent of men and 15 percent of women admitted to having extramarital affairs in their marriages. While there has been a slight increase in this data, monogamy is practiced in most of the marriages in America. Heterosexual men commit to a monogamous relationship with their wives—not because they do not desire to have sex with other women, but rather because they have a strong sense of integrity. Most adult men and women have a sense of honesty and values that make them feel it is wrong to have an affair. They have awareness that it would be very hurtful to their partner. They also know that it would be a violation that would make them feel guilty about what they did. For many married men and women, it is just wrong. They are committed to being monogamous, and they will not break that promise.

Tom and Jackie have been monogamous together during the thirty-one years they have been married. It appears that the majority of married couples in America maintain monogamy in their marriages. Infidelity only has to be dealt with in a minority of American marriages. Infidelity is very hurtful and sometimes destructive to a marriage. It destroys the trust in the relationship. It undermines the self-esteem of the offended party. It is humiliating. In many cases, it puts an end to the marriage. For some people, it is an offense so hurtful that they cannot stay in the relationship.

Bill and Jane have been married eleven years. They had a child their third year of marriage and another child their fifth year of marriage. Before they had children, they had a very good sex life together. They remember having sex five times or more a week. With the birth of their first child, their sexual relationship started to change. Jane was tired from working and taking care of the baby. She felt exhausted almost every night. Sex just seemed like another chore she had to do before she could get to sleep. They started to have less sex. With the birth of their second child, things changed dramatically. Their sex life all but stopped completely. Something else happened.

Bill felt that Jane was spending all her time caring for the children, but not caring for him. He felt that Jane's time and her thoughts were all about the children. It seemed that all she could talk about was the children. She only became excited when the children did something cute or funny that she wanted to share. Bill came to the realization that Jane had emotionally divorced him and married their children. The children came first in everything. All the spare time she had was spent talking and playing with the children. All she wanted to talk about with Bill was the children. The only time he felt any approval from Jane was when he would play with the children. He felt angry at Jane and started to withdraw. It seemed that Jane did not even care. Bill started feeling all she wanted was children, and that was the only reason she married him. Whenever he would try to tell her what he was feeling, she would get angry at him. Jane would go through a long list of the things she had to do, and say how tired she was and how Bill was not helping enough. She would attack him with comments about how he did not appreciate her and all that she was doing.

Jane would go to bed right after she put the children to bed. Bill would spend most evenings alone. He started staying up late watching pornography. He then got on a porn chat site. He started communicating with a woman who sounded interested in him. It was not too long before Bill discovered that this sexy woman he was talking with lived right in his own town. He made a date with her, and they met one night after work for a drink. He told Jane he had to work late. The woman's name was Susan. She was very attracted to Bill, and he was very attracted to her. They started a sexual relationship. It was not too long before Jane noticed that Bill was acting strangely. He was working late almost every night. On the weekends, he often had to go back to the office. At home, he acted tired all the time. He did not talk much to her anymore. He did not have much sexual interest in her. In fact, when she would ask him if he would like to have sex, he would say that he was too tired.

In a conversation with some of her girlfriends, Jane mentioned how tired Bill was and how hard he was working. Her women friends became very suspicious that Bill was having an affair. They told Jane to check up on Bill. While Bill was gone, she checked his e-mail on his computer and found the evidence that confirmed that her girlfriends were right.

Jane was shocked. She could not believe that Bill could do such a thing. The hurt cut through her like a knife. She felt a rush of anger. She felt she had to leave him, yet she knew she still loved him. She now felt a total distrust of him. She felt confusion because she loved him, but she hated him for what he had done. She wanted him to leave immediately, and at the same time, she did not want him to go. She waited for Bill to come home. When he did, she had dozens of questions: "How long has this affair been going on?" "Do you love her?" "Have you had other affairs?" "Why did you do this?" "How could you do this to me?" "Did you tell her anything about me?" "Where does she live?"

The questions kept coming. They were repetitive. Jane tried to make sense out of her confusion. She could not believe Bill would do this to her and his family. Bill did not know what to say. He felt guilty, sorry, apologetic, and ashamed. He kept telling Jane that he loved her and would do anything to keep their marriage. He said he was willing to get marriage counseling.

When Bill and Jane went to the marriage counselor, they learned that they needed to work on a number of issues. They had to deal with all the feelings created by Bill's affair. Jane had to sort out all her feelings and decide if she was going to divorce Bill or try to work things out. They also had to address what the issues were in their relationship before Bill's affair.

Dualism, Distance, Dishonesty, and Infidelity

When people are involved in a clandestine affair, they suffer from living a dualistic life. They are actually living two lives. One is with their partner with whom they are in marriage, and the other is with their paramour with whom they are involved in an affair. They have to hide their lover from their partner. Time spent seeing their lover is time away from their partner as well as their family life. Finding time to be with their paramour often involves making up lies and being dishonest. Thinking about the person you are involved with as well as spending time with them puts more distance between you and your partner. This often makes the marriage more difficult. Over time, the capacity for duplicity erodes one's sense of integrity, which is perhaps the most insidious problem. Most importantly, the third party becomes a distraction from confronting the issues in the marriage.

There are cases when an affair can be helpful to people who are not in love with their partner. They know they want out of the relationship, but they are not psychologically strong enough to be able to leave. Often getting involved in an affair gives them the confidence and support to leave a bad marriage or relationship. For them, an affair is helpful. In some cases, getting involved with someone else can bring you to a deeper realization of the importance of your current partner. In such cases, the cheating partner stops the affair and turns the focus on his or her partner again. There are couples that fall back in love again in the process of dealing with an infidelity, but in my experience of working with couples dealing with this issue, most of them suffer permanent damage that never seems repairable.

Infidelity Can Destroy the Feeling of Love

There are couples that cannot work out the damage done when one of them has become involved with someone else. I have known both men and women who, upon learning of their partner having an affair, immediately contact an attorney and file for divorce. For these people, they cannot ever forgive or forget the hurt the affair caused them to feel. The relationship has been killed. I have observed couples that spend as much as two years in marriage counseling, trying to heal the hurt, anger, and distrust that an affair creates. At the end of the counseling, the offended party files for divorce. Often they feel that they cannot heal from the hurt as long as they stay in the marriage.

I have known couples that stay together after an infidelity, but the feeling of being in love is gone. The trust and respect the offended party once had for the offending spouse has been scuttled. They often stay together for the children. Sometimes they cannot afford a divorce. They stay together, but it is never the same. Often religious beliefs that do not permit divorce as an option keep a couple together, but the level of damage felt is too severe to ever restore the feeling of love. For some couples the hurt never leaves, and the lost love and trust never returns.

The Process of Healing an Infidelity

How do couples heal from an infidelity? The healing involves a process that can help repair the damage done, if a couple can follow it. A couple must deal with the feelings they had between them before the start of the affair and the feelings they now feel since the discovery of the affair. It is doubtful a couple with a close emotional connection can allow a third party to come between them. The issues they had before the start of an affair disconnected them. Had they addressed those issues, there may not have been an infidelity. The unaddressed problems often contribute to the reason for the affair. Once the affair is discovered, they need to address this crisis in their relationship. Because of the complexity of having to work out issues on two different levels, before the affair and after the affair, it is often helpful for a couple to seek out a competent marriage counselor to help them.

Discussing the "before and after" feelings and issues is an important part of the healing process. The offended party often feels that things were good between them when the affair started. In some cases, the offended party was not aware of the problems, or knew there were issues but did not feel they were that serious. Often the offending party has not been direct or honest with their spouse about dissatisfaction in the marriage. In some cases, both had been in denial of the problems existing between them.

What I have found that is important to the healing process is the need for the offended partner to be able to express their hurt, anger, and distrust to their spouse over and over again. This process is redundant. The hurt partner needs to repetitively ask the same questions and repetitively express the same feelings they have about the affair. If their offending spouse can understand the need for repetitious expression over weeks and months of the pain they have caused, often the relationship starts to improve. This "working out" process is really a form of desensitization. Repetitive discussion of the feelings can wear them out, and it can desensitize them so that they become less and less a topic of discussion.

What is most difficult in this process is the reaction of the partner who had the affair. They feel that because they have discussed the affair several times it should be resolved. They have given an apology, and the details of the event have been made transparent. A promise of commitment and love has been assured, so why should a couple keep talking about it? They need to understand that the healing process is redundant so that feelings can be exhausted, worked out, and worn out. This requires patience, understanding, and empathy on the part of the offending partner. Even though you have answered all the questions multiple times, this repeated verbosity wears the issue out and helps in the healing.

Infidelity Can Be Worked Out and the Relationship Improved

Many couples can resolve the suffering and distrust created by an affair. The affair opens up honest communication at a level they had never known together. Going through the process of healing from the affair improves their relationship and gives them a more intimate connection. They begin to feel closer than they were before the affair happened. These couples, years later, feel that although it was awful, it was the best thing that ever happened to their relationship. They not only learned a lot, but their relationship improved because of that experience. They learned to communicate more honestly and more directly. They learned to listen to each other and to make time to keep in contact.

Couples need to learn to live in the present and not in the past. The focus should be in the here and now, not in what happened years ago. If they can create meaning and pleasure in the here and now, they will feel a connection that transcends some painful event in the past.

I have also observed that when a married person no longer loves their spouse and wants a divorce, getting involved in an affair can be very helpful; especially when they do not have the psychological strength to leave. An affair can give a person the support and confidence to leave a marriage that is no longer right for them.

The Infidelity Prevention Formula

There is a formula for the prevention of infidelity. If a couple was to make a joint effort to follow this formula, they would have almost 100 percent protection against either partner getting involved with a third party. Consider how Tom and Jackie managed to be together thirty-one years without any infidelity. When you compare Tom and Jackie's marriage to that of Bill and Jane's, you can see major differences between these two marriages. Tom and Jackie follow the infidelity prevention formula, and Bill and Jane do not. Here is a review of what Tom and Jackie do to keep fidelity in their relationship.

1) They allow and respect each other's independence and personal freedom. They give each other space to do what each likes to do. They do not get in each other's way. They support each other's private meanings. There is a wide margin of freedom in the relationship for them to do what they like to do without their partner. It is not expected that they have to do everything

together. Each of them supports the fact that they have an independent private life within their marriage.

2) No one in the relationship has dominant control of the other. There is no boss in this marriage. They work at maintaining a peer relationship. Each respects the other's feelings. When they disagree, they negotiate through the difference together, with no one dictating the solution. All solutions have to be agreeable to both of them.

3) They follow the rules of good communication. They both actively listen to each other. When one of them is talking, the other does not interrupt. Each of them waits for their turn to express what they are feeling. All feelings and points of view are respected and considered. Differences are negotiated to a place where both can agree. They do not attack each other's self-esteem with labeling and name-calling. They understand that in a disagreement no one is right or wrong in how they see it. They see the issue differently, and they negotiate and compromise to come to an agreement that is satisfying to both of them.

4) They are very open about their sexuality. They have rid themselves of sexual fears, guilt, shame, and embarrassment. They have not only developed an openness in talking about sex, but they are able to share with each other their most personal and private sexual feelings. They have rid themselves of most of their inhibitions. They have an understanding that sex can be a lighthearted activity that is mostly erotic fun, or it can be a serious and emotionally intense, intimate event. Both of them are comfortable having sex with themselves. Masturbation is an accepted and expected ongoing practice with both of them. Pornography is also accepted as a visual aphrodisiac and is not considered threatening or necessarily private. They both understand male sexuality and the high levels of sexual tension that males have to manage. They maintain an active sex life with each other and can talk openly and freely about any sexual needs or feelings either of them may have. Sex alone is not enough glue to keep a couple together, but sexual conflict can inspire infidelity and divorce.

5) They use the language of endearment in their communication. Both of them flood their communication to each other with positive compliments and many "I love you" messages. They understand how important positive reinforcement is to their relationship. They both pay attention

for opportunities to give each other support, compliments, help, and love. They have learned to speak affectionately to each other. In addition, they give each other a lot of nonsexual physical touch. When sitting on the sofa while watching television, one of them will give a foot rub to the other. At night when they get in bed, one of them will massage the other's shoulders or back. They always hug and kiss good-bye and greet each other with a hug. Sometimes when they are passing by each other in the living room or down a hallway, they will reach out and touch. It is a common practice for either of them to look the other straight in the face, smile, and say, "I love you." They look for ways to give each other validation.

6) Tom and Jackie are very aware of their attractions to other people. They know that the idea that there is just one man for each woman and one woman for each man is complete nonsense. They believe there are thousands of compatible partners for everyone. Occasionally they both know they are going to meet one of those "also compatible" partners. When they do, they will feel the rapport, affinity, and physical attraction. While they recognize they would like to get involved with this attractive person, upon this recognition they set the boundary immediately. Neither of them ever flirts, because they both know that flirting suggests that you are available to get involved if the other party is willing. They also do not confide personal feelings to someone else that should only belong to their relationship. They never tell this attractive person anything they have not shared with each other. Lastly, Tom and Jackie talk and laugh about other people that they find attractive. This is not a threatening conversation, because they always validate what they love about each other and about being together.

7) Tom and Jackie have an agreement about feeling sexual. They agree that they can be turned on by other people or by fantasies of sex with others; be that through pictures, thoughts, or a real person. They have made a commitment: they are to fulfill all sexual feelings by having sex with oneself or with each other. They are very clear about their agreement to be sexually exclusive, which for them means absolutely no physical contact that is sexual with anyone, but that does not apply to what and how they become turned on.

Couples who work on these seven areas in their marriages will develop a deeper and stronger bond against infidelity. However, this formula for the prevention of infidelity does not work with all couples. There are some individuals, both male and female, whose personalities are borderline, sociopathic, or narcissistic. These psychological conditions keep them from maintaining boundaries. They are often so self-centered and needy that they cannot maintain fidelity or integrity. It is rare that psychotherapy can help them, nor will marriage counseling. They have a form of mental illness that is usually therapy proof. For these couples, their marriages are doomed to chronic misery or divorce. Couples who sign a marriage license and have a wedding are not necessarily married. They are only married on paper, but they often have not emotionally married each other. A couple can go through a wedding ceremony and sign a marriage license, but that does not make them married. It is only when a couple feels a deep emotional, psychological, spiritual, and physical connection that they are truly married. It is easy to stray in a marriage when you are not really married. When the emotional commitment has not been established, but only vocalized, the relationship is vulnerable to a third party involvement.

When we make the decision to marry someone, we are putting limits on our life. Actually, if you consider it, all decisions rule out other choices and limit your life. If I make a decision to head south, I have ruled out being able to go north, east, or west. When I marry and agree to be sexually exclusive with my partner, I am ruling out having sex with anyone else. I am putting limits on my sexual experiences. I will be having sex with this one person for the rest of my life. However, consider what you also gain. No other relationship provides the opportunity to learn more about oneself than does the marital relationship; you become known as you are known by no other person on earth, which includes both the wonderful parts of your personality as well as the dark side of you. You will have constant support throughout your lifetime. You will have a helpmate to make your life easier. You will never really be alone. You will have someone to do things with any time of the day or night. You will have someone to share the enormity of life. You will have a person who gives you love and receives your love. You will have a continued opportunity for sexual satisfaction. You will build a shared history, which provides great comfort in your aging years. You will have someone for whom you never have to put on that social mask to have acceptance. When your health is giving you problems, you will have a partner who gives a damn for you and will be there for you. If you and your partner want to have children and create a family, that in itself is a unique experience that can be fulfilling, far more than getting laid two thousand times.

The reality of our lives involves far more than just having sex. We need confidence, meaning, acceptance, love, support, understanding, and someone to help share the struggle of life. We need medical care and a career that can support us. Most of all we need social connection. Birds fly in a flock; cattle are in a herd; fish swim in schools; and humans have always had connection to a tribe. To be in a relationship with someone is important to most people. Marriage has the potential to connect us to a partner, as well as a social culture, which seems very important to mental health and good psychological adjustment in life. I recognize that marriage is not for everyone, nor should everyone have children. Living together with someone can also give many of these benefits without a marriage. For most people marriage can fulfill a deep primary need that is basic to existence. Early in the social development of human life, male and female coupled up and created family. Marriage is a social recognition within a culture of that coupling.

Conclusion

Breaking Free of the Negative Sexual Script and Living More Erotically

According to Webster's Dictionary, the word "hoodwink" means to deceive, delude, dupe, mislead, bamboozle, or snow. The negative sexual script advocates have hoodwinked the American people. A large segment of our population has been taught to feel guilt, shame, and fear about our natural sexuality. The erotophobes have deluded parents to fear teaching sex to their children. Parents have been duped into thinking it is better not to give positive sexual information to children. They wrongly feel that ignorance is better than comprehensive sex education. It is a well-known fact that most children in all other industrialized countries have comprehensive sex education. Abstinence from sex until you get married is not taught, but being responsible sexually is taught. Other industrialized countries also provide information on contraception. They make contraceptives readily available to teenagers. In America, we do not, and we have the highest teen birth rate among all other industrialized countries. Is it right to support fourteen-, fifteen-, and sixteen-year-old children having children?

Our Congress earmarks more than two hundred million tax dollars per year to promote abstinence as the sexual script for America. Until recently, they had bamboozled the Department of Education to withhold federal funding from any state that does not follow the negative scripting of abstinence from sex until marriage and abstinence of all information on the subjects of birth control and condom usage. Even more negatively, schools that receive federal funding for education are required to teach that sex outside of marriage is harmful to one's psychological health. They have also demonized the fine work done by Planned Parenthood. Planned Parenthood is one of the places where one can get honest, accurate, and comprehensive sex education, but the negative sexual script advocates have made people afraid to use their services. We have abundant research studies from our finest universities that confirm that a first-century Christian teaching on sexuality does not work in the twenty-first century. This scripting from the first century and the Middle Ages has had a negative effect on our sexuality. It has contributed to the inhibition, guilt, and fear people have of allowing erotica in their lives. It is also responsible for the sexual frustration so many couples have in their marriages.

At the university where I teach human sexuality, I ask my students what they think is America's official sexual script. They talk about how sexy America is and all the sexual freedom there is in this culture. However, when I hand them a test on sexual anatomy, only a few nursing students can pass it. If I ask how they feel about masturbation, there is a majority negative response. Most of that negative response is from the women. How many of them enjoy oral sex? A small minority. Sexual positions? The majority prefer the man on top.

Then I place on the overhead projector the sex laws of the fifty states. I emphasize Idaho's sex laws against having sex outside of marriage; its "crimes against nature" laws that make any oral or anal genital contact a crime. I read them the law that makes adultery a crime. I show them similar laws in the other forty-nine states. They are shocked, to say the least. They want to know how these laws, which seem so ridiculous, ever get on the law books. I tell them that the term "crimes against nature" was coined by Saint Thomas Aquinas in the thirteenth century; that the teachings about sex in first-century Christianity is funded by our tax dollars and promoted by our federal and state government and most of the churches in America. They feel they have sexual freedom, but many of them are dealing with sexual frustration and inhibition.

I hear men complain how much their partners reject them when they put moves on them for sex. I hear complaints from female partners about how mechanical their sex life feels. I hear confessions from clients that they feel little sexual desire for their partners. There are many males that cannot share erotica with their female partner, so they hide the fact that they like viewing it. I keep hearing from women who feel they should never think outside of the box when it comes to sexuality and hardly think about the subject, with the exception of when they are servicing their husbands.

What has happened to their erotic dimension? Where is their lust? Have they disconnected from their natural mating urge?

I ask my students, "How many of you are feminists?" The majority of the class gives a negative response. I remind them that if it was not for feminists, none of the women would be able to attend college. They would not be sitting in this classroom. They would all grow up to be housewives and uneducated mothers of children. Their husbands would be the head of the family, which means their roles would be to submit to their husbands' wishes. I tell the women in the class that if it was not for the feminists, a woman could never be a senator, a congresswoman, or a governor of a state. I place on the overhead projector all the other countries that have elected women to the highest political office, president of the country. I remind them that we here in the United States have not yet achieved this, even though the majority of voters in this country are women. I ask them why this is so. Why do women in America make less than men for the same work? Double standard? Why is a woman still viewed as less of a person than a man? The negative sexual script advocates feel that there are clear gender roles, which are different for women than they are for men. That first-century view is still in vogue here in America.

I remind the men that all the responsibility to pay for everything would be on them, because their wives would not have careers. I remind them that if it was not for the feminists, none of the women would be able to vote in America's elections. I tell them that the Roman Catholic Church opposed and helped keep contraception illegal in the United States. Margaret Sanger smuggled diaphragms into America from France and gave them freely to women, many of whom had ten to fourteen children or more. Sanger was arrested, but she still managed to start a movement to legalize contraception in the United States.[157] She eventually was successful and founded Planned Parenthood to provide contraception and comprehensive sex education. She was opposed by the negative sexual script advocates then, and her work is still opposed by them now. How would the men in class appreciate having to support twelve children and a wife?

How do the men in class feel about having a wife who feels guilty about sex, and who only does it for him, but is not interested in it for herself? Women often feel guilty about their sexuality. Many women are uncomfortable about experimentation with different sexual positions, different forms of stimulation, and deep erotic states. Many women are still uncomfortable letting their husbands see them in the nude. Orgasm is difficult for a large segment of women.

Feminists are primarily responsible for the sexual liberation of women. The negative sexual script advocates oppose feminism as unholy and wrong. What is a feminist? A feminist is anyone who cares about women having equal rights. This is an example of how the negative sexual script promoters, through misinformation, have convinced countless numbers of our citizens that feminism is something that is destructive.

It seems ironic that any woman would not be a feminist. Feminism is responsible for women having full citizenship as men have. How can women not appreciate feminism? The negative sexual script advocates have promoted the misinformation and propaganda to turn women against the very movement that has liberated them from a "Taliban" type of existence in society. It has taken federal law enforcement for them to even get and keep their equal rights. Until the passage of the Nineteenth Amendment in 1920, women were disenfranchised in America.

When the students first come to class, they think they know everything about sex. They are in denial. I am their instructor, and I would be the first to tell you that I do not know everything about sex. The students are amazed when I tell them that the withdrawal method of birth control does not work and is very risky. Why? Because of the Cowper's gland. This is a little gland in the male that secretes a cleaning fluid when a male becomes erected. When a man gets an erection, the Cowper's gland secretes a fluid that goes down the urethra and neutralizes any urinary acids. Its purpose is to clean and prepare the urinary canal for the sperm. Often, in this clear or slightly white fluid, there are living sperm. Although the male has not ejaculated, the woman gets pregnant from the fluid of the Cowper's gland. How many teenagers become pregnant because they do not have this information? Important information like this is not being taught in almost all sexuality classes in American high schools. We are not allowed, or we are afraid, or we just do not know enough information to properly teach young people how to have sex.

I have been counseling couples for almost forty years. I have found that countless couples are having sexual difficulty in their relationship. Although we have sex all around us in this culture, sex is still one of the primary problems for many couples. We see sexual images in advertising in almost every magazine. We have sex scenes in almost all movies rated R, and television is saturated with sexual advertising: sexual movies, comedians talking explicitly about sex, and sitcoms with sex scenes. We also recently have seen programs such as *Sex in the City* and *Hung* on HBO television. So, while it seems that our culture is sexually competent and open, how is it that so many couples struggle with sexual problems and issues? Males struggle with performance issues about getting and keeping an erection, and women struggle with the lack of sexual desire and satisfaction of achieving orgasm. Couples are inhibited and uncomfortable with erotica and deep erotic states. They are uncomfortable with erotic language. So much of what is good erotica is viewed by American women as dirty.

Pornography, the kind that is not degrading to a man or a woman, is just erotica. Porn is recognition of our animal nature. It is showing a couple completely focused on the mating urge. It is about our natural drive to procreate. Porn shows us pure erotica with no complications of a relationship, no performance pressure, no problems with sexual dysfunction, no rules, nothing that is sexually wrong. Porn is about humans in an erotic state, people in sexual heat. In pornography, we see humans acting out their basic biological nature. The women want it as much as the men. Together, the man and the woman do everything to give pleasure and to stimulate each other to orgasm. The male is giving pleasure to the female and the female is giving pleasure to the male. Both get into a deep erotic state where each of them becomes focused on pleasure.

There is no sexual frustration in porn; there is no guilt, no shame, no inhibition, and no sexual restriction. Both the male and the female know exactly what to do to achieve maximum pleasure with each other. In porn, the man says, "Suck my dick," and the woman sucks his dick. In so many marriages, the husband knows there is no point in even asking. In porn, the woman says, "Eat my cunt," and the man licks her clitoris. In so many marriages, the wife knows her husband does not like to go down there. Too often, the wife does not like to have oral stimulation, even if her husband wants to do that for her. Why would a female not enjoy a soft wet tongue stroking her clitoris? Because Aquinas said it was sinful? Because there are state sodomy laws against doing that kind of stimulation? Because it is embarrassing to show too much vulnerability? Because she is just trying to please her husband, not herself? Alternatively, is it that she just does not feel comfortable getting too hot? So many women have been conditioned to view erotica as dirty and awful. No wonder having an orgasm is so difficult for so many women. Could their inhibitions inspire their husbands to view porn?

In porn, the male holds off until the female comes and is satisfied. In so many marriages, the male comes first and the female is left unsatisfied. Would the wife then masturbate in front of her husband or teach him how to masturbate her? The women in the porn movies will. Given the erotic nature of males (remember males have twenty to forty times the amount of testosterone in their blood than females) and the difficulty so many women have with feeling a desire for sex, it is not surprising that men find porn easier, simpler, and in many cases more real and enjoyable than having sex with their uptight and rule-bound partner.

Explain to me why so many women have difficulty viewing porn? I often hear women complain that if their husband watches porn, it is no different than him having an affair with another woman. The only woman who should be on his mind is his wife. Doesn't that sound like the corrupted interpretation of the lust verse from Matthew, chapter five? Why can't she watch porn with her husband and let it turn her on? I am certain her reasons for not watching will come right out of the negative sexual script promoter's playbook. "It isn't love; it is lust." "The male is using that female." "The female has been manipulated by males to do what she is doing." "That female is a whore, and I am not a whore." "I don't think it is right; they are just acting. Real life sex and real life women are not that way." Is it true that real life sex is not like a couple that is acting in a porn movie? Why not? Why isn't it? The fact is that there are women who are sexually liberated and who do respond sexually like a porn star.

One answer I have heard from some women about the erotica seen in porn movies is that sex is not supposed to be for pleasure, but for love. So if you do it for love, then it is not as open, free, and pleasurable. If porn shows us anything, it shows us what erotica looks like. When you surrender to your lust, to your erotic feelings, you will not only feel deep pleasure, but you will also give deep pleasure to your partner. Most men would not prefer sexual fantasy to having sex with a real, live erotic partner.

I am amazed at the sexual ignorance men have about women and women have about men. Sexuality is at the epicenter of our biology. Our sexuality is a part of our nature. It is natural. It was with us when we walked on all fours as it is with us now. It should be easy, and it should be fun. It most certainly should be pleasurable. Is the problem that the negative sexual script advocates have achieved their goal of repressing, inhibiting, and restricting sexual enjoyment? Are we so embarrassed about our sexuality that we cannot talk about it openly with the person we love and live with? The person we sleep next to, eat with, and share everything with, the person we have built a life with? Couples cannot talk about their sexual feelings or needs with the person to whom they have committed to be sexually exclusive. When it comes to the subject of sex, too many of us have guilt, shame, fear of masturbation, and discomfort with oral stimulation, the rear entry position, the use of vibrators or sexual toys, talking about it, viewing it, reading about it, and teaching it. All of these are problematic issues in our culture. We have been deceived; we have been deluded, tricked, bamboozled, hyped, snowed. We have been hoodwinked! We have been hoodwinked by the negative sexual script invented by a group of individuals, authorities, and institutions. They have invented this script because of their guilt, fear, and shame. They have for centuries projected their unnatural, fearful, and abnormal negative fears on sex. They have written a script they want us all to use as the sexual standard. They are the erotophobes who fear their natural sexuality. While other Western nations seem to have evolved beyond their corrupted sexual views, America is still listening to them and believing them. It is as if we are voting against ourselves.

Making your marriage more erotic is a process of rejecting the negative sexual script and becoming liberated from the conventional assumptions you have been taught about sexuality. When a couple can view sex, read explicit sexual books and magazines, and allow themselves to discuss their sexual feelings and desires openly, their marriage or relationship will become more erotic. By allowing erotic language and lustful expression into their relationship, a couple will not only experience more pleasure and sexual freedom together, they will also feel more connected and bonded. Making a continual effort to court and romance each other will enhance both a sexual and an emotional relationship that is unbreakable and exclusive.

Endnotes

[1] Tannahill, Reay. "Sex in History." pp. 160-169. 1982. Stein and Day, New York, NY Baur, Karla., Crooks, Robert. "Our Sexuality" p. 10-12, Eleventh edition. 2008/2011. Thomsen-Wadsworth, Belmont, CA.

[2] Baur, Karla., Crooks, Robert. "Our Sexuality" p. 408, Eleventh edition. 2008/2011. Thomsen-Wadsworth, Belmont, CA.

[3] Kegel, Arnold, American Institute of Family Relations, Internship Training Seminar, Fall 1967. Los Angeles, CA.

[4] *Ladies Home Journal*, "Can This Marriage Be Saved?" December 1968.

Chapter One

[5] Goodman, Ellen. *Seattle Times*, July 19, 1996.

[6] CNN.com. "Beaten Gay Student Dies: Murder Charges Planned." October 12, 1998

[7] Klein, Marty. "America's War on Sex." pp. 11–13, 2006, Praeger Publishers, Westport, CT. Apuzzo, Matt, Reuters.com, "Abstinence Vows, Risk Taking Tied." Associated Press, Saturday March 19, 2005.

[8] Berne, Eric. "Games People Play." pp. 32–35, 1964. Grove Press, New York, NY.

[9] *Merriam-Webster's New Dictionary and Thesaurus*, 2002. Wiley Publishing, Cleveland, OH.

[10] Baur, Karla, Crooks, Robert. "Our Sexuality" pp. 11–12. Eleventh Edition. 2008/2011. Thomsen-Wadsworth, Belmont, CA.

[11] Cott, Jonathan. "Isis and Osiris: Exploring the Goddess Myth." pp. 27–31. 1994. Doubleday, New York, NY.

[12] ibid.

[13] ibid.

[14] The Holy Bible, The Old Testament, Revised Standard Version. Genesis Chapter 3:1–24. Revised 1952. Thomas Nelson & Sons, New York, NY.

[15] Tannahill, Reay. "Sex in History." pp. 141–142. 1982. Stein and Day, New York, NY Baur, Karla, Crooks, Robert. "Our Sexuality." pp. 11–12. 2008/2011 Eleventh Edition. Thomsen-Wadsworth, Belmont, CA.

[16] The Holy Bible, The Old Testament. Revised Standard Version. Genesis Chapters 3:1–21. Revised 1952. Thomas Nelsen & Sons, New York, NY.

[17] Aquinas, Saint Thomas. "Summa Theologica." Translation by the Fathers of the English Dominican Province. 1947. Bensinger Brothers, New York, NY.

[18] Baur, Karka, Crooks, Robert, "Our Sexuality." pp. 11–12. Eleventh Edition. 2008/2011. Thomsen-Wadsworth, Belmont, CA.

[19] Cott, Jonathan. "Isis and Osiris: Exploring the Goddess Myth." pp. 7–24. 1994. Doubleday, New York, NY.

[20] The Holy Bible, The Old Testament, Revised Standard Version. Genesis Chapter 3:1–24. Revised 1952. Thomas Nelsen & Sons, New York, NY.

[21] Cott, Jonathan. "Isis and Osiris: Exploring the Goddess Myth." pp. 7–24. 1994. Doubleday, New York, NY.

[22] The Holy Bible, The Old Testament, Revised Standard Version. Genesis Chapter 3:1–24. Revised 1952. Thomas Nelsen & Sons, New York, NY.

[23] Baur, Karla, Crooks, Robert. "Our Sexuality." pp. 10–12. 2008/2011. Eleventh Edition. Thomsen-Wadsworth, Belmont, CA.

[24] Boswell, J. "Same Sex Unions in Pre-Modern Europe." pp. 74. 1994. Villard Publishing, New York, NY. Westheimer, Ruth K., Lopater, Sanford. "Human Sexuality." pp. 31–38. 2005. Lippincott Williams & Wilkins, Baltimore, MD.

[25] Bernstein, Richard. "The East, the West, and Sex." pp. 38–39. 2009. Alfred A. Knopf, New York, NY.

[26] ibid.

[27] ibid.

[28] Freeman, Charles. "The Closing of the Western Mind." pp. 395–640. 2005. Vintage Books, New York, NY. Tannahill, Reay. "Sex in History." pp. 141–142. 1982. Stein and Day. New York, NY.

[29] Baur, Karla, Crooks, Robert. "Our Sexuality." pp. 11–12. 2008/2011 Eleventh Edition. Thomsen-Wadsworth. Belmont, CA.

[30] The Holy Bible, The New Testament, Revised Standard Version. Corinthians Chapter 7:1. Revised 1952. Thomas Nelsen and Sons, New York, NY.

[31] Baur, Karla, Crooks, Robert. "Our Sexuality." pp. 10–12. 2008/2011. Eleventh Edition. Thomsen-Wadsworth, Belmont, CA.

[32] ibid.

[33] Baur, Karla, Crooks, Robert. "Our Sexuality." pp. 266. 2008/2011. Eleventh Edition. Thomsen-Wadsworth, Belmont, CA.

[34] ibid.

[35] ibid.

[36] Yahoo! Search, 2010. "Is Oral Sex Illegal in the United States?"

[37] ibid., "Is Fornication Illegal in the United States?"

[38] ibid., "Is Adultery Illegal in the United States?"

[39] ibid., "Is Heterosexual Anal Sex Illegal in the United States?"

[40] Wikipedia, 2003. "Sodomy Laws in the United States: Lawrence vs. Texas."

[41] Google Search, 2010. "Felony Sodomy Law Reinstated in Idaho."

[42] Guttmacher Institute.org. "Facts on Sex Education in the United States." 2006. CBS News, "States Rejecting Abstinence-only Funding." Washington, Jan. 7, 2008. Alagiri, J. D., Priya, Collins, Chris, M. P. P., Summers, Todd, "Abstinence Only vs. Comprehensive Sex Education." Policy Monograph Series, March 2002.

[43] Freeman, Charles. "The Closing of the Western Mind." pp. 395–640. 2005. Vintage Books, New York, NY, Baur, Karla, Crooks, Robert, "Our Sexuality." pp. 10–13. 2008/2011. Eleventh Edition. Thomsen-Wadsworth, Belmont, CA.

[44] Nova, "Galileo's Battle for the Heavens." Nova Online home page. 2002. Kelly, Kathryn, Bryne, Donn, "Exploring Human Sexuality." p. 15. 1992. Prentice-Hall, Englewood Cliffs, NJ.

[45] Caron, Sandra L., PhD. "Sex Around the World: Cross-Culture Perspectives on Human Sexuality." pp. 125–128. 2007. Pearson Custom Publishing, Boston, MA.

[46] Sipe, Richard A. W. "A Secret World: Sexuality and the Search for Celibacy." 1990. Brunnel/Mazel, New York, NY.

[47] Collinson, Patrick. "The Reformation: A History." pp. 178–182. 2004. Modern Library Edition, Modern Library, www.modernlibrary.com.

[48] Baur, Karla, Crooks, Robert. "Our Sexuality." p. 12. 2008/2011. Thomsen-Wadsworth, Belmont, CA.

[49] ibid.

[50] Hill, Craig A. "Human Sexuality." pp. 70–72. 2008. Sage Publications, Thousand Oaks, CA. Rowan, Edward L, MD. "The Joy of Self-Pleasuring." pp. 11–127. Prometheus Books, Amherst, NJ. Kellogg, J. F. "Plain Facts

for Old and Young." pp. 231–259. 1891 Segner & Company, Alanta, GA. Jefferis, B. G., Nichols, J. L. "Safe Counsel." pp. 294–346, 438–440. 1922. J. L. Nichols & Company, Naperville, IL.

51 Buar, Karla, Crooks, Robert. "Our Sexuality." p. 15. 2008/2011 Eleventh Edition. Thomsen-Wadsworth, Belmont, CA.

52 ibid., p. 16.

53 Pomeroy, Wardell B. "Dr. Kinsey and the Institute for Sex Research." pp. 313, 333–334. 1972. Harper & Row, New York, NY. Baur, Karla, Crooks, Robert. "Our Sexuality." p.408. 2008/2011. Eleventh Edition. Thomsen-Wadsworth, Belmont, CA.

54 ibid.

55 Watts, Steven. "Mr. Playboy: Hugh Hefner and the American Dream." pp. 64–65, 80. 2008. John Wiley & Sons, Hoboken, NJ.

56 Baur, Karla, Crooks, Robert. "Our Sexuality." p. 40. 2008/2011. Eleventh Edition. Thomsen-Wadsworth, Belmont, CA.

Chapter Two

57 ibid., p. 555

58 CNN.com. "Bush 'disappointed' by Gay Marriage Ban's Defeat." Thursday July 15, 2004. Baur, Karla, Crooks, Robert. "Our Sexuality." pp. 25, 264, 283, 303, 323, 325, 485, 557. 2008/2011. Eleventh Edition. Thomsen-Wadsworth, Belmont, CA.

59 The Holy Bible, The Old Testament, Revised Standard Version, Revised 1952. Thomas Nelsen & Sons, New York, NY.

60 ibid.

61 ibid.

62 ibid.

63 ibid.

64 ibid.

65 ibid.

66 ibid.

67ibid.

68 ibid.

69 ibid.

70 The Holy Bible, The New Testament. Revised Standard Version, Revised 1952. Thomas Nelsen & Sons, New York, NY.

71 ibid.

72 ibid.

73 ibid.

74 ibid.

75 ibid.

76 ibid.

77 The Holy Bible, The New Testament. Revised Standard Version. Revised 1952. Thomas Nelsen & Sons, New York, NY.

78 Pope John Paul II. *Philadelphia Inquirer.* p. 3. Oct. 8, 1980.

79 Scheer, Robert. "The Playboy Interview: Jimmy Carter." *Playboy Magazine.* Nov. 1976, Volume 23, Issue 11, pp. 63–68.

80 The Holy Bible, The New Testament. Revised Standard Version. Revised 1952. Thomas-Nelsen & Sons, New York, NY.

81 ibid.

82 ibid., Matthew 23:13–35.

83 ibid., Matthew 22:39, Mark 12:31.

Chapter Three

84 Baur, Karla, Crooks, Robert. "Our Sexuality." p.12. 2008/2011. Eleventh Edition. Thomsen-Wadsworth, Belmont, CA.

85 *Merriam-Webster's New Dictionary and Thesaurus.* 2002. Wiley Publishing Company, Cleveland, OH.

86 Baur, Karla, Crooks, Robert. "Our Sexuality." p. 40. 2008/2011. Eleventh Edition. Thomsen-Wadsworth, Belmont, CA.

87 ibid., pp.164–168.

88 Davis, Murray S. "Smut: Erotic Reality/Obscene Ideology." pp. 1–11. 1983. University of Chicago Press, Chicago, IL.

89 Baur, Karla, Crooks, Robert. "Our Sexuality." p. 164. 2008/2011. Eleventh Edition, Thomsen-Wadsworth, Belmont, CA.

Chapter Four

90 Meshorer, Mac and Judith. "Ultimate Pleasure: The Secrets of Easily Orgasmic Women." pp. 25–35, 1986. Saint Martin's Press, New York, NY.

91 Caron, Sandra L. "Sex around the World." pp. 178–180. 2007. Pearson Custom Publishing, Boston, MA.

92 ibid., pp. 125–128.

93 Tanenbaum, Leora. "Slut: Growing Up Female with a Bad Reputation." pp. 7–28, 37–40. 2000. HarperCollins Publishers, New York, NY.

[94] Ehrenreich, Barbara, et al. "Re-making Love: The Feminization of Sex." pp. 74–102, 1987. Doubleday, New York, NY. Baur, Karla, Crooks, Robert. "Our Sexuality." p. 408. 2008/2011. Eleventh Edition. Thomsen-Wadsworth, Belmont, CA.

[95] Baur, Karla, Crooks, Robert. "Our Sexuality." pp. 29, 169. 2008/2011. Eleventh Edition. Thomsen-Wadsworth, Belmont, CA.

[96] Robinson, Marie N., MD. "The Power of Sexual Surrender." p. 58. ff. 1958. Doubleday, New York, NY.

[97] ibid.

[98] Kegel, Arnold, MD. Lecture Seminar at The American Institute of Family Relations. 1968. Los Angeles, CA.

[99] ibid.

[100] ibid.

[101] ibid., Zilbergeld, B. "Male Sexuality: A Guide to Sexual Fulfillment." p. 109. 1978. Little Brown Publishers, Boston, MA.

[102] Kegel, Arnold, MD. Lecture Seminar at the American Institute of Family Relations. Internship Training Program. 1968. Los Angeles, CA.

[103] Carroll, Janell, L. "Sexuality Now." p. 292. 2005. Wadsworth-Thomsen, Belmont, CA.

[104] Masters and Johnson. Training Seminar in Sexual Dysfunction, Oct. 4–5, 1977. Las Vegas, NV.

[105] Westheimer, Ruth, K., Lopater, Sanford. "The G Spot." p. 241. 2005. Lippincott, Williams, and Wilkins, Baltimore, MD.

[106] Baur, Karla, Crooks, Robert. "Our Sexuality." pp. 61, 169–170. 2008/2011. Eleventh Edition, Thomsen-Wadsworth, Belmont, CA.

[107] Masters and Johnson. Training Seminar in Sexual Dysfunction, Oct.4–5, 1977. Las Vegas, NV.

[108] Baur, Karla, Crooks, Robert. "Our Sexuality." pp. 11–12. 2008/2011. Eleventh Edition, Thomsen-Wadsworth, Belmont, CA. Tanenbaum, Leora. "Slut: Growing Up Female with a Bad Reputation." pp. 7–28, 37–40. 2000. Harper Collins Publishers, New York, NY.

Chapter Five

[109] Rowan, Edward L., MD. "The Joy of Self-Pleasuring." pp. 102–103. 2000. Prometheus Books, Amherst, NY.

[110] Wikipedia, The Free Encyclopdia. "Joyceln Elders."

[111] Rowan, Edward L., MD. "The Joy of Sexual-Pleasuring." p. 113. 2000. Prometheus Books, Amherst, NY.

[112] ibid., p. 97.

[113] ibid., p.113–114.

[114] ibid., p.113–114. Stengers, Jean, Van Neck, Anne. "Masturbation: The History of a Great Terror." pp. 77–80. 2001. Palgrave Press, New York, NY.

[115] Jefferis, B. G., Nichols, J. L., "Safe Counsel." pp. 294–346, 438–440. 1922. J. L. Nichols & Company, New York, NY.

[116] Rowan, Edward L., MD. "The Joy of Self-Pleasuring." p. 114. 2000. Prometheus Books, Amherst, NY.

[117] ibid., p.118.

[118] ibid., p.118.

[119] ibid., p.120.

[120] ibid., p. 122–123.

[121] Jones, James H. "Alfred Kinsey." pp. 580–600.

[122] Masters and Johnson. Training Seminar in Sexual Dysfunction. Oct. 4–5, 1977. Las Vegas, NV.

[123] Google.com. "Prostate Massage and Health."

[124] Baur, Karla, Crooks, Robert. "Our Sexuality." p. 514. 2008/2011. Eleventh Edition, Thomsen-Wadsworth, Belmont, CA. D'Amato, Anthony. "Porn Up, Rape Down." June 23, 2006, Northwestern Public Law Research Paper No. 913013. Northwestern University School of Law. Social Science Research Network.

[125] Kreisler, Kristin Von. "The Healing Powers of Sex." *Redbook,* April 1993. New York, NY.

[126] ibid.

Chapter Six

[127] Brill, A. A., Dr. "The Basic Writings of Sigmund Freud." p. 592. 1938, Random House, New York, NY.

[128] Rock, Chris. "The Chris Rock Rule of Fidelity." Laughing man, Oct.15, 2003.

[129] Baur, Karla, Crooks, Robert. "Our Sexuality." pp. 556–558. 2008/2011. Eleventh Edition, Thomsen-Wadsworth, Belmont, CA. American Online. com. Pornographic Statistics, 2006.

[130] Kinsey, Alfred C., Pomeroy, Wardell B., "Dr. Kinsey and the Institute for Sex Research." pp. 313, 333–334. 1972. Harper & Row Publishers, New York, NY. Weinberg, Martin. "Sex Research Studies from the Kinsey Institute." p. 60. 1976. Oxford University Press, New York, NY. Carroll,

Janell L. "Sexuality Now." pp. 291–292. 2005. Wadsworth/Thomsen, Belmont, CA.

[131] American Psychiatric Association. "DSM-5 Development." 2010. Arlington, VA. APA@psych.org.

[132] Carnes, Patrick J., PhD, Carnes, Stephanie, PhD. "Understanding Cybersex in 2010." *Family Therapy Magazine.* pp. 10–16, Jan/Feb 2010.

[133] Carroll, Janell L. "Sexually Now." pp. 519–520. 2005. Wadsworth-Thomsen, Belmont, CA.

[134] Hyde, Janet Shibley, Delamater, John D. "Understanding Human Sexuality." pp. 404–405. 2006. McGraw-Hill, New York, NY.

[135] Carnes, Patrick J., PhD, Carnes, Stephanie, PhD. "Understanding Cybersex in 2010." *Family Therapy Magazine,* pp. 10–16, Jan/Feb 2010.

[136] ibid.

[137] Klein, Marty, PhD. "America's War on Sex: The Attack on Lust, Law, and Liberty." pp. 1–4. 2006. Praeger Publishers, Westport, CT.

[138] Baur, Karla, Crooks, Robert. "Our Sexuality." p. 516. 2008/2011. Eleventh Edition, Thomsen-Wadsworth, Belmont, CA.

[139] Lajeunesse, Simon Louis, PhD. "Pornography's Effect on Men Under Study." University of Montreal, 2009, Google, Psychcentral.com.

[140] ibid., Baur, Karla, Crooks, Robert. "Our Sexuality." p. 558. 2008/2010. Eleventh Edion, Thomsen-Wadsworth, Belmont, CA. Greenberg, Jerrold S., Bruess, Clint E., Conklin, C. "Exploring the Dimensions of Human Sexuality." p. 764. 2007. Third Edition, Jones and Bartlett Publishers, Sudbury, MA.

[141] ibid., pp. 554.

[142] Nevid, Jeffery S., Fichner, Lois, Rathus, Spencer A. "Human Sexuality in a World of Diversity." pp. 635–642. 1995. Second Edition, Simon & Schuster Company, Needham Heights, MA.

[143] Karolides, Nicholas J., Bald, Margaret, Sova, Dawn B. "100 Banned Books." pp. 268–289. 1999. Checkmark Books, New York, NY.

[144] McKee, Alan; Albury, Katherine; Lumby, Catherine The Porn Report Melbourne University Press 2008

[145] Donnerstein, Edward, Linz, Daniel, Penrod, Steven. "The Question of Pornography: Research Findings and Policy Implications." pp. 61–66, 108–130. 1987. Free Press, Macmillian, Inc., New York, NY. Featherstone, Liza. "Porn." 2005. *Psychology Today,* Sept/Oct. Lajeunesse, Simon Louise, PhD. "Pornography's Effect on Men Under Study." 2009. University of Montreal, Psychcentral Group, Google. Society for the Scientific Study of Sexuality., "What Sexual Scientists Know About Pornography." 2005.

[146] Baur, Karla, Crooks, Robert. "Our Sexuality." p. 159. 2880/2010. Eleventh Edition, Thomsen-Wadsworth, Belmont, CA.

[147] Baur, Karla, Crooks, Robert. "Our Sexuality." p. 83. 2008/2010. Eleventh Edition, Thomsen-Wadsworth, Belmont, CA.

Chapter Seven

[148] Gottman, John M., PhD. "The Seven Principles of Making a Marriage Work." p. 102–103. 1999. Three Rivers Press, New York, NY.

[149] Ministry of Integration and Gender Equality. Government Office of Sweden. Publication October 2009. "Equal Rights and Opportunities Regardless of Sexual Orientation or Transgender identity or Expression." Bennhold, Katrin. "The Female Factor: Men Can Have It All." June 9, 2010. *New York Times.*

[150] Caron, Sandra, PhD. "Sex Around the World: Cross-Culture Perspectives on Human Sexuality." p. 177. 2007. Pearson Custom Publishing, Boston, MA. Wikipedia.org, "Prostitution in Sweden." 2010.

[151] About.com. Women's History. "Women Prime Ministers and Presidents, Heads of State." Twentieth Century.

[152] Joyce, Amy. "Women Severely Underrepresented in Fortune 500 Companies." *Washington Post*, August 6, 2006.

[153] Caron, Sandra L. "Sex Around the World: Cross-Culture Perspectives on Human Sexuality." 2007. Pearson Custom Publishing, Boston, MA.

[154] ibid.

[155] Gottman, John, M., PhD. "The Seven Principles of Making a Marriage Work." p. 103. 1999. Three Rivers Press, New York, NY.

[156] Barbach, L. *For Yourself: The Fulfilment of Female Sexuality* (1976, REV. 2000) Anchor Press. Garden City, N.Y.

[157] Moglia, Ronald, Filiberti, Ed D., Knowles, Jon. "All about Sex: A Family Resource on Sex and Sexuality." p. xix, Introduction. 1997. Three Rivers Press, New York, NY.

CPSIA information can be obtained at www.ICGtesting.com
Printed in the USA
241639LV00007B/134/P